P9-CDT-270

The Epic of
Gilgamesh

THE EPIC OF GILGAMESH

"Then fortune smiled so fully on my acts
 that I began, at 3:00 a.m. beneath a swollen moon,
to intone an epic, being first antiphonarion once again,
 as I'd been when a boy in noble,
holy woods surrounded by my brothers
 and sure that God had callen me
to speak for Him."

DEDICATION

for Bak Shar
whose death gave birth
to this

The Great Books Foundation has developed questions and discussion guidelines for *The Epic of Gilgamesh.*

These questions and discussion guidlines are available from:

www.bolchazy.com/Assets/Bolchazy/extras/GreatBooksQuestions.pdf

Questions from **GREAT CONVERSATIONS I,** by the Great Books Foundation.
Copyright (c) 2008 by the Great Books Foundation.
Reprinted by permission of the Great Books Foundation.

THE EPIC OF
GILGAMESH

Verse rendition by
Danny P. Jackson

Introduction by
Robert D. Biggs

Appreciation by
James G. Keenan

Illustrated by
Thom Kapheim

BOLCHAZY-CARDUCCI PUBLISHERS

General Editor
Laurie Haight Keenan

Cover Design
Charlene M. Hernandez

Typography
Kay McGinnis Ritter

Cover Illustration
Thom Kapheim
Figure 25: The Bull

The Epic of Gilgamesh

Danny P. Jackson

© 1997 Bolchazy-Carducci Publishers, Inc.
All rights reserved

Bolchazy-Carducci Publishers, Inc.
1570 Baskin Road
Mundelein, Illinois 60060 USA
www.bolchazy.com

Printed in the United States of America
2015
by United Graphics

ISBN 978-0-86516-352-2

Second Edition

Revised 1992 Edition
Last figure indicates year of this printing:
2013 2012 2009 2008 2005 2004 2000 1997

Library of Congress Cataloging-in-Publication Data

Gilgamesh. English.
The epic of Gilgamesh / verse rendition by Danny P. Jackson ; introduction by Robert D. Biggs ; an appreciation by James G. Keenan ; illustrated by Thom Kapheim. -- 2nd ed.
    p.   cm.
Includes bibliographical references.
ISBN 0-86516-352-9 (softcover : alk. paper)
1. Epic poetry. Assyro-Babylonian -- Translations into English.
I. Jackson, Danny P., 1946-   . II. Title
PJ3771.G5E5   1997
892'. 1--DC21

                                      97-25048
                                         CIP

TABLE OF CONTENTS

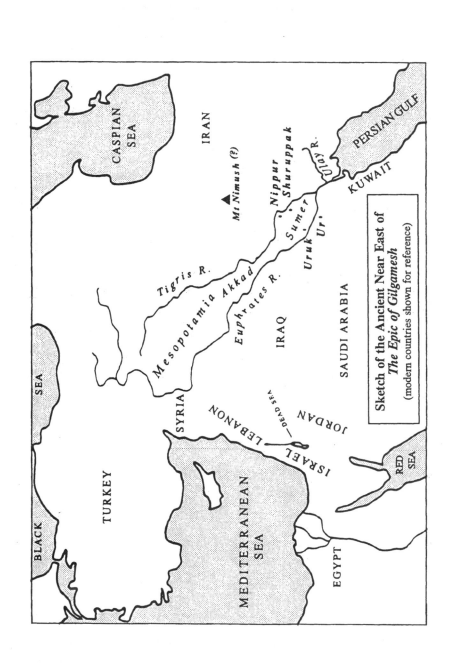

Sketch of the Ancient Near East of
The Epic of Gilgamesh
(modern countries shown for reference)

LIST OF ILLUSTRATIONS
From the Ancient World
(pp. XIII – XXX)

Figure

1. Fragment of Tablet XI in Assyrian cuneiform.
Copyright © British Museum.

2. Head of Ashurbanipal, from a limestone panel detail.
Copyright © British Museum.

3. Reed house, detail from stone trough relief.
Copyright © British Museum.

4. Photo of miniature boat model from Ur.
Negative #S8-22100, courtesy of the University Museum, University of Pennsylvania.

5. Man and woman at banquet, depicted on gypsum plaque.
Photo courtesy of The Oriental Institute of The University of Chicago.

6. Ziggurat at Warka (ancient Uruk).
Photo #622.5037, courtesy of Hirmer Verlag, Munich.

7. Ziggurat at Ur during 1930s excavations.
Photo reproduced from Ur Excavations: Vol. 5, *The Ziggurat and its Surroundings*, Sir Leonard Woolley's account of the 1939 joint expedition of the British Museum and the University of Pennsylvania to Mesopotamia.

8. Artist's drawing of suggested reconstruction of Ziggurat at Ur.
Photo reproduced from Ur Excavations: Vol. 5, *The Ziggurat and its Surroundings*, Sir Leonard Woolley's account of the 1939 joint expedition of the British Museum and the University of Pennsylvania to Mesopotamia.

9. Four-faced god and goddess.
Photo courtesy of The Oriental Institute of The University of Chicago.

10. Sumerian stone statue.
Photo courtesy of The Oriental Institute of The University of Chicago.

11. Stone relief from Tell Halaf.
Photo #21.12, courtesy of the Walters Art Gallery, Baltimore.

12. Scene engraved on copper vessel.
Photo #10.823, courtesy of Hirmer Verlag, Munich.

13. Modern rolling of Assyrian cylinder seal from the first millennium B.C.
Photo #686, courtesy of the Pierpont Morgan Library, New York.

14. Figures on a gold bowl from Hasanlu, Iran.
Negative #S8-96557, courtesy of the University Museum, University of Pennsylvania.

Original Artwork by Thom Kapheim

PUBLISHER'S PREFACE

I first learned of *Gilgamesh* in 1967. As a practicing Catholic and former seminarian, I wondered why I hadn't been informed that other ancient cultures told the same stories pondering the same human condition as the Hebrew stories in Genesis: Adam and Eve, Paradise Lost, and the Great Flood came to life in the tablets of the *Epic of Gilgamesh* in haunting similarity to the Biblical accounts. I was fascinated with this first extant epic, this first hero, this first set of parallels to—in fact, predecessors of—the Bible.

As a man, I could empathize with the stages in Gilgamesh's journey, his coming of age, his rites of passage: the unbridled libido yielding to the social drive to produce something of fame; the realization that self-satisfaction is not truly satisfying, that in a mature relationship a new whole is born of two and is richer and deeper than either one; bereavement giving birth to the sheer terror of one's own mortality; the wasted aerobics of body and soul aimed at foiling the grim reaper, even if only for a few more years; finally, the resignation and mustering of courage to accept one's natural limitations, making the best of the here and now without any expectations beyond this life. All of these stages are mapped out along the road Gilgamesh follows.

My fascination with *Gilgamesh* led me to teach it at every opportunity. I felt, however, that the available translations made the story inaccessible to many readers. As a publisher, I addressed the problems: lacunae and notations made them unreadable; prose renditions lacked epic grandeur. Danny Jackson's rendition is, for me, both poetic and accessible—the readable version this fascinating tale deserves. Modern scholarship under Robert D. Biggs and new illustrations by Thom Kapheim give added value.

The impetus for a second edition—with introductory material expanded by Robert Biggs and James Keenan, and revisions to the text by Danny Jackson—came from our readers. A different Kapheim illustration graces the cover: it is a turning point in the epic when the rejected Ishtar releases the Bull of Heaven. Gilgamesh and Enkidu kill the Bull, but it in turn mortally wounds Enkidu. The death of Enkidu drives Gilgamesh to search for immortality and to discover the meaning of mortal life. Shortly after the grief-stricken Gilgamesh begins his quest, he is received in the cottage of the hospitable Siduri. It is she who answers the epic's thematic question: "What is best for us to do?"

The answer is not the Christian "other-worldly" beatific vision, nor the Stoic *pietas* that leads to final amalgamation with the fiery *logos*, nor the *ataraxia* of Epicurus and Lucretius, nor the *eudaimonia* of Aristotle. The answer given to Gilgamesh is closer to the Homeric answer. Quite simply, it is to be the best human possible, to reject the various utopias, dowries of kingdoms and immortality; instead, to press on from one goal to another; to give scope to brawn, both physical and intellectual, and to appetites. For just as Shamhat, by means of her sacrament of Ishtar, leads Enkidu away from his feral existence into the city of human beings, so also Siduri with her advice points Gilgamesh away from his paradisal hope of divinity and immortality toward acceptance of his humanity; in short, to make the best of his lot.

This is the threshold of a new stage in Gilgamesh's life. Not yet able to accept his mortality, he resorts to "religion." He falls back on the words of Siduri only when religion fails him, after he loses the herb of immortality to the serpent at the pool of water. It is the first recorded conversion, the first baptism of water making a passage from the mythological to the real, from a pursuit of immortality and divinity to acceptance of human nature and its corollary, death. He will be "new born," a convert. He will, if he follows Siduri's advice, seek a wife and not a goddess, enjoy his children and his people, not the company of gods. He will build immortal walls rather than seek everlasting life. This new life of becoming perfect according to human nature is in antithesis to becoming perfect beyond nature as a divinity.

The final illustration in the book (figure 33) shows Gilgamesh, a "new man," resigned to his limitations and resolved to make the best of what nature provides. While the fear of death shook him to the marrow, it will no longer spoil the good that life can offer. Gilgamesh has arrived at the last stage of a journey to find life's meaning. At what stage are you?

Ladislaus J. Bolchazy
2000

INTRODUCTION

Much of the ancient world's literature has perished and, if it survives at all, it is known from excerpts quoted by ancient authors or from scraps of papyrus found in Egypt. Most of the works of even such a famous writer as Euripides have been lost, and we are surely fortunate to have eighteen intact plays out of about ninety that he is known to have written. Others survive as mere fragments. We lament still the loss of the great Library of Alexandria. There are occasional finds of manuscripts that have survived, of which the Dead Sea Scrolls is one of the most famous. There are a few others such as the Papyrus House at Herculaneum where the papyrus scrolls were carbonized in the eruption of Mount Vesuvius in A.D. 79. These scrolls largely await scientific conservation techniques that may recover ancient works of philosophy and literature.

Ancient Mesopotamia—the Land Between the Two Rivers—presents a contrast to the Classical world whose traditions were kept alive over the centuries. The ancient cultures of Mesopotamia were largely unknown and only dim memories survived to modern times in such writers as Berossos, a Babylonian priest writing in Greek, whose works are known only from the works of others who happened to quote him. Some individuals and some historical events are known from passages in the Bible. All this changed with the nineteenth century rediscovery of ancient Assyria (the northern part of modern Iraq). This is not the place to report the saga of the decipherment of the complicated cuneiform script, so called because of the wedge-shaped (Latin *cuneo*, "wedge") signs. Suffice it to say that by 1850, there was general agreement among scholars who had studied it that it had been successfully deciphered and that the cuneiform texts could, by and large, be read and understood.

Nineveh, ancient capital of Assyria, whose exact location had long been forgotten, was in fact discovered in the mound known as Kouyunjik across the Tigris from the modern city of Mosul. The British excavators had the good fortune to come upon huge numbers of broken clay tablets that were eventually identified as being the remains of the library of the last Assyrian king, Assurbanipal. Apparently the clay tablets were deliberately broken to bits when Nineveh was sacked in 612 B.C. But unlike the scrolls in Alexandria, many of the clay tablets, though broken and chipped, survived in the ground until discovered in modern times. Other parts of the library, inscribed on wooden boards covered with wax, which we know of from various library records, have perished completely.[1]

In 1872, a young British scholar, George Smith, who was studying these tablets at the British Museum, startled literary and religious circles in England when he announced that one of these fragments told about a boat being built, a great flood, a bird being released to seek dry land as the flood receded, and a man and his wife who survived the flood. The discovery was perceived to be of such significance that it was arranged for Smith to announce it at a public lecture attended by Prime Minister Gladstone, on December 3, 1872.[2] Here was the Babylonian Noah! One modern author (Jack Sasson) has commented that the flood narrative shocked Europe no less than any of Darwin's theories, for it placed into question the uniqueness and authenticity of Scripture.

But, alas! Smith had found only a fragment of a tablet. Popular excitement was such that a newspaper, the *Daily Telegraph,* provided funds to send Smith back to Nineveh to seek other parts of the tablet. By a great stroke of luck, he found another fragment concerning the Flood. When he announced this discovery to the newspaper, its management seemed satisfied that the mission had been completed and asked Smith to return to England. We know now, however, that the fragment he found at Nineveh was not a part of the *Gilgamesh Epic,* but rather a piece of a related flood story, the *Atra-hasis Epic.*

Babylonian works of literature, medical texts, collections of omens, and other scholarly compilations were divided into what we would normally call chapters, but which the Babylonian scholars called Tablets (*ṭuppu*). Each had a number, but, unlike our chapter headings, the information was given at the end in a colophon (such a colophon usually included the name by which the work was known,

---

1   Parpola, "Assyrian Library Records."
2   Walker, "The Kouyunjik Collection," p. 185.

but sometimes included information on the source of the manuscript it was copied from, the name of the scribe, and sometimes the date when it was copied). And since works of literature were generally known by their first lines, the *Epic of Gilgamesh* was known as "He who saw everything" (Babylonian *ša nagba īmuru*). Thus, for example, at the end of Tablet VI, we find *tuppu* 6.KAM *ša nag-ba e-mu-ru*, "Tablet VI of He Who Saw Everything."[3] What is often called the Standard Version of the *Epic of Gilgamesh*[4] consists of twelve such tablets or chapters, with the flood story being part of the eleventh. The most usual format of the actual cuneiform tablets is six columns of writing, three on the front, or obverse, and three on the back, or reverse, of the tablet, with the sequence of columns being left to right on the obverse and right to left on the reverse (cuneiform tablets turn top to bottom rather than side to side like our books so that column iv—the first column on the reverse—is adjacent to column iii of the obverse). Unlike the scripts for related languages such as Hebrew and Arabic, cuneiform script is read from left to right.

Surely future archaeological work will bring to light further fragments of the *Gilgamesh Epic*, but for the present, there remain substantial gaps, and a number of episodes are only partially known. Fortunately, scribes and scholars in different cities and towns owned copies of various tablets of the epic, and, by combining the texts from different sources, it has been possible for modern scholars to make a reasonably complete edition of some of the tablets. For example, Tablets I and XI are nearly complete when the various fragmentary sources are combined. A new scholarly edition of the cuneiform texts,

---

3　We are not absolutely certain of the meaning of the opening words. Some scholars have preferred to read instead of *nagba*, "everything," *naqba*, "the Deep" (the cuneiform script does not distinguish between the two words, and while in most instances the choice is obvious from the context, that is not necessarily the case for the *Gilgamesh Epic*). From what we know of the episodes in the epic, both would seem appropriate. It may even be that, as often in poetry, the ambiguity was intentional, and we are intended to understand both. There are a number of other intentional ambiguities and plays on words that cannot readily be shown in translation.

4　It is called "standard" because it is the version datable to the first millennium B.C. found at a number of ancient sites and which are identical in sequence of episodes, division into "Tablets," and wording.

with transliterations and translations, is in preparation by Andrew R. George of the University of London. This edition, incorporating a considerable number of newly discovered manuscripts, will be the first such edition of all the cuneiform texts since Reginald Campbell Thompson's of 1930.

Preceding the Standard Version of the first millennium B.C. was another version, referred to as the Old Babylonian Version. Some episodes are preserved only in the Old Babylonian Version, and translators normally combine the two for the sake of making a coherent story.

The Literary Sources of the *Gilgamesh Epic*

Various versions of the *Gilgamesh Epic* seem to have circulated widely in the second millennium B.C. and are found as far west as the Hittite capital of Hattusha in central Anatolia, modern Turkey. Another fragment was found at the ancient Palestinian site of Megiddo. It is the twelve-tablet version, sometimes called the Standard Version, that is best known. Even though sources have been found at widely scattered sites in Mesopotamia and Anatolia, the text seems largely standardized, with most variants being insignificant spelling variations (which are perfectly normal in the cuneiform writing system) or occasional small differences in wording. Tablet XII seems to be almost a literal translation of the Sumerian composition "Gilgamesh, Enkidu, and the Netherworld" and it has often been argued that it does not really belong to the epic at all! One major translation of the Epic omits Tablet XII entirely. Others argue that Tablet XII is an essential part of the Standard Version. (See the article of Vulpe cited in the Further Reading section below.)

In the days before copyright law assured literary ownership of one's written word or one's musical compositions, borrowing and adaptations were common. So it was with the *Gilgamesh Epic* and other works of Sumerian or Babylonian literature.

The major Sumerian sources relating to *Gilgamesh* are the following: "Gilgamesh and Agga of Kish," "Gilgamesh, Huwawa, and the Cedar Forest," "Gilgamesh and the Bull of Heaven," and "Gilgamesh, Enkidu, and the Netherworld."

The episodes of "Gilgamesh and Agga" have no direct counterpart in the Standard Version. "Gilgamesh, Huwawa, and the Cedar Forest," on the other hand, provides the basis for Tablets IV and V of the Standard Version. "Gilgamesh and the Bull of Heaven" has been only partly recovered so we do not yet know all the details of the Sumerian account. It is the source for the Standard Version's Tablet VI.

As Piotr Michalowski points out, by the end of the second millennium B.C. historical and legendary figures had been transformed into authors of fictional autobiographies; the great transformation to fictional autobiography took place when the Standard Version of *Gilgamesh* was created. A prologue was added that turned the whole story into a third-person autobiography, thus changing the whole narrative.[5]

We do not know how much else was added at this point, but the flood story, taken from another composition that dealt with the figure of Atra-hasis, was probably among the additions. The main function of the flood story is really to insert a story within a story. As Michalowski observes, "This is the autobiography of Uta-napishtim and as such it directs Gilgamesh to the ultimate end of his quest: he will achieve immortality only through the epic itself because his immortal fame will only be a function of the tale that he will write down with his own hand. That, of course, leads back to the beginning of the text—in Sin-leqe-unninni's version—to the fact that the whole composition is an elaborate *narû*, a gigantic royal inscription.... The Gilgamesh text is narrated in the third person, is ascribed to an author named Sin-leqe-unninni, but is actually treated as a third-person autobiography of Gilgamesh."[6]

As mentioned above, ancient Babylonian scholars attributed authorship of *Gilgamesh* to a man named Sin-leqe-unninni, a scholar-scribe in Uruk who probably lived in the Middle Babylonian period (about 1300 B.C.), and it may well be that he was indeed the editor or compiler of the twelve-tablet version now referred to as the Standard Version.[7] But whoever the compiler or compilers may have been, they

5   Michalowski, pp. 188–89.
6   Michalowski, p. 188.
7   See Laurie E. Pearce, "The Scribes and Scholars of Ancient
    Mesopotamia," in Jack M. Sasson, ed., *Civilizations of the Ancient Near
    East* (New York, 1995), vol. 4, pp. 2265–78, esp. p. 2275.

drew upon old Mesopotamian literary traditions, including a number of episodes that have survived in Sumerian as separate tales. This is true for the Old Babylonian sources we have as well as the late version.

The Historical Background of the Epic

The hero of the story, Gilgamesh, was a ruler of Uruk, one of the famous old cities in southern Mesopotamia. We are uncertain whether he was an actual ruler of Uruk or not, even though the Sumerian King List attributes to him a reign of 126 years in the First Dynasty of Uruk. (The name "Gilgamesh," however, is of a type typical of the period in which he supposedly lived.)

It has to be admitted, however, that no original inscriptions of Gilgamesh have come to light, though we do have a few original inscriptions of rulers of Kish and Ur who are associated with Gilgamesh in later literary and historical traditions (the Sumerian literary text "Gilgamesh and Agga," for example). According to literary tradition, the mother of Gilgamesh was the goddess Ninsun, whose spouse was Lugal-banda, an earlier king of Uruk. There is a Sumerian literary text from about 2600 B.C. that is a dialogue between Lugal-banda and Ninsun. Gilgamesh is not mentioned in the dialogue, but this text takes us within a couple of generations of the time Gilgamesh is thought to have lived.[8] We may not get any closer to contemporaneity with figures—real or legendary—associated with Gilgamesh than this.

Eroticism in the *Gilgamesh Epic*

The *Gilgamesh Epic* is ripe with themes reflecting the human condition, including the universal awareness of our own mortality. (For more on this theme, see James Keenan's appreciation, below.) Another aspect of the epic that has received considerable attention by modern commentators and scholars is the erotic elements.

Part of the debate on sexuality and eroticism in *Gilgamesh* concerns the interpretation we feel entitled to give to certain episodes. There is,

8   See Thorkild Jacobsen, "Lugalbanda and Ninsuna," *Journal of Cuneiform Studies* 41 (1989) 69–86.

of course, little ambiguity in the passage concerning Shamhat's ardent sexual encounter with Enkidu, one stage of his passage to humanness. In vivid language, often rendered less explicit in translations, the poet describes the activity. (See Danny Jackson's discussion, below.)

Quite the opposite is the case with the poet's description of the relationship between Gilgamesh and Enkidu. Many authors have believed evidence for a homosexual relationship between the two men can be found in these passages, which are couched in poetic imagery that leaves room for various interpretations. It seems inappropriate, in any case, to apply the modern European concept of homosexuality to an ancient text. Benjamin Foster writes of the friendship between Gilgamesh and Enkidu, which, in his view, has no sexual basis at all, and adds, "This union seems the closer for being asexual and of near equals."[9] It is true, of course, that most of the erotic imagery occurs in the dream episodes and not in the accounts of the adventures Gilgamesh and Enkidu share.

We are fortunate, therefore, to have the dream episodes preserved in both the Old Babylonian version and the Standard Version.[10] In the first dream, in the Old Babylonian version, Gilgamesh tells his mother, the wise goddess Ninsun, what he has dreamt, saying that he saw the sky and that something like a meteorite fell near him. He tried to lift it, but could not. The people of Uruk gathered around it, kissing its feet as if it were a baby. He loved it and embraced it as he would a wife, and then he set it before his mother, and she "made it equal" to him.[11] Then she interprets the dream for him, saying that a strong companion will come to him, that he is mighty, strong as a meteorite, that he loved him and embraced him as a wife. She ends, saying, "Your dream is favorable and precious." The Standard Version has a shorter explanation of the dream (though not all preserved). The mother of Gilgamesh, predicting the appearance of Enkidu, tells him that one like him has been born on the plain and the mountains have raised him. "You will see him and rejoice. Young men will kiss

---

9   Foster, "Gilgamesh, Sex, Love and the Ascent of Knowledge," p. 22.

10 See especially Cooper's study cited in the "For Further Reading" section. This section on the dreams is heavily indebted to Cooper's interpretation.

11 The expression, "make him your equal" seems to imply that Ninsun will treat Enkidu as a son.

his feet. You will hug him. [Here there is a small break.] You will bring him to me."

In the second dream, he reports that he saw an ax had fallen and people were gathered around it. He put it in front of his mother, saying, "I loved it and embraced it as a wife, and then you 'made it equal' to me." She explains the dream: "A strong companion will come to you, who rescues his friend; strongest in the land, he is mighty. His might is as strong as a meteorite." In the Standard Version, he says he saw the ax and rejoiced, loved it and embraced it as a wife,[12] but then says, in what is obviously an intentional pun or ambiguity playing on the fact that the word *ahu* means both "side" and "brother," either "I took it and placed it at my side" or "I took it and made it a brother." It may be worth noting that Gilgamesh repeatedly refers to Enkidu as his "brother," though whether this is to be understood as a family relationship or social equality we cannot be sure.

Decisions of Editors/Translators

Any translator or editor of an ancient text must make a number of decisions in presenting a translation to modern readers who are necessarily unfamiliar with the conceptual framework within which the work arose.[13] (See also the discussions of Jackson and Keenan in this volume.)

In the past, one well-known English translation of the *Gilgamesh*

---

12 The Akkadian term translated here as "embrace" in some contexts is clearly a euphemism for sexual intercourse, and it may be in our passage as well. But there is some ambiguity. Both the Old Babylonian version and the Standard Version say explicitly "embrace him/it as a wife." However, in the Babylonian potency incantations and rituals dealing with sexual intercourse, the word·for "wife" is never used; instead, the word for "woman" is used. The significance of the use of the word "wife" (instead of "woman") in both the Old Babylonian version and the Standard Version might be that the meaning of "embrace him/it as a wife" in these passages refers to affectionate embraces and not necessarily sexual intercourse.

13 A most obvious case is the names of ancient deities or historical persons who were quite familiar to the original audience. The case of Shamash (*Šamaš*) is an example, where a translation can say simply "the Sun God," and where Sîn can be called "the Moon God." Other deities may require an explanation.

Epic (that of Alexander Heidel) switched to Latin for the erotic episodes. Other translators used euphemisms to avoid a straightforward translation that some readers might find offensive. (See detailed comments by Jackson below on this specific topic.)

A special problem is what to call the woman who brings Enkidu to his sexual awakening. Some call her "the prostitute" or "the harlot." To my mind, this gives a misleading and erroneous impression. The woman is called Shamhat. This is a form of the Babylonian verb *šamāhu*, "to grow thickly or abundantly (said of vegetation), to flourish, to attain extraordinary beauty or stature." Part of the problem is that there is a noun *šamhatu* that the ancient Babylonian scholars grouped with other nouns representing certain women connected with temples. The function of these women is poorly understood, but some scholars have believed they may have had some sexual role. There is no evidence in Babylonian texts that there was anything shameful about *šamhatu*. In fact, in a recently-published document of the Old Babylonian period (early second millennium B.C.) we find a woman bearing the name Nanaya-šamhat. Nanaya was one of the Babylonian goddesses of love, and I suspect that the name means something like "The-Goddess-Nanaya-is-Voluptuous." If so, Shamhat might be called "She-Who-Is-Voluptuous."

The *Epic of Gilgamesh*, even though we have not recovered it in its entirety and some episodes remain incomplete or enigmatic, is a literary masterpiece capable of speaking to us over the centuries of our human condition. As the Alewife says to Gilgamesh in the Old Babylonian version

> When the gods created mankind,
> For mankind they allotted death.
> Eternal life they kept for themselves.

Robert D. Biggs
The Oriental Institute
of The University of Chicago

For Further Reading

Bendt Alster, "Lugalbanda and the Early Epic Tradition in Mesopotamia," in Tzvi Abusch, John Huehnergard, and Piotr Steinkeller, eds., *Lingering over Words: Studies in Ancient Near Eastern Literature in Honor of William L. Moran* (Atlanta, 1990), pp. 59–72.

C. Collard, M. J. Cropp, and K. H. Lee, eds., *Euripides: Selected Fragmentary Plays*, vol. 1 (Warminster, 1995).

Jerrold S. Cooper, "Gilgamesh Dreams of Enkidu: The Evolution and Dilution of Narrative," in Maria de Jong Ellis, ed., *Essays on the Ancient Near East in Memory of Jacob Joel Finkelstein* (Hamden, Connecticut, 1977), pp. 39–44.

Benjamin Foster, "Gilgamesh: Sex, Love and the Ascent of Knowledge," in John H. Marks and Robert M. Good, eds., *Love and Death in the Ancient Near East: Essays in Honor of Marvin H. Pope* (Guilford, Connecticut, 1987), pp. 21–42. Reprinted in John Maier, ed., *Gilgamesh: A Reader* (Wauconda, IL, 1997).

Benjamin Foster, "On Authorship in Akkadian Literature," *Annali* (University of Naples) 51 (1991) 17–32.

Alexander Heidel, *The Gilgamesh Epic and Old Testament Parallels*, second edition (Chicago, 1949).

Thorkild Jacobsen, *The Sumerian King List*, Assyriological Studies 11 (Chicago, 1939)

Thorkild Jacobsen, "Lugalbanda and Ninsuna," *Journal of Cuneiform Studies* 41 (1989) 69–86.

Thorkild Jacobsen, "The Gilgamesh Epic: Romantic and Tragic Vision," in Tzvi Abusch, John Huehnergard, and Piotr Steinkeller, eds., *Lingering over Words: Studies in Ancient Near Eastern Literature in Honor of William L. Moran* (Atlanta, 1990), pp. 231–49.

Dina Katz, *Gilgamesh and Akka* (Groningen, 1993).

Anne D. Kilmer, "Crossing the Waters of Death: The 'Stone Things' in the Gilgamesh Epic," *Wiener Zeitschrift für die Kunde des Morgenlandes* 86 (1996) 213–17. [Suggests that the "stone things" were kedges, a sort of anchor which, when lodged in the earth in shallow water, can be used to pull a boat forward—as opposed to punting poles, which are means to push a boat forward.]

W. G. Lambert, "A Catalogue of Texts and Authors," *Journal of Cuneiform Studies* 16 (1962) 59–77.

W. G. Lambert, "Gilgamesh in Literature and Art: The Second and First Millennia," in Ann Farkas et al., eds., *Monsters and Demons in the Ancient and Medieval Worlds* (Mainz, 1987), pp. 37–52. Reprinted in John Maier, ed., *Gilgamesh: A Reader* (Wauconda, IL, 1997).

W. G. Lambert and A. R. Millard, *Atra-ḫasīs: The Babylonian Story of the Flood* (Oxford, 1969).

Benno Landsberger, "Scribal Concepts of Education," in Carl H. Kraeling and Robert M. Adams, eds., *City Invincible: A Symposium on Urbanization and Cultural Development in the Ancient Near East Held at the Oriental Institute of the University of Chicago, December 4–7, 1958* (Chicago, 1960), pp. 94–102.

Mogens Trolle Larsen, *The Conquest of Assyria: Excavations in an Antique Land 1840–1860* (London and New York, 1996).

Piotr Michalowski, "Sailing to Babylon, Reading the Dark Side of the Moon," in Jerrold S. Cooper and Glenn M. Schwartz, eds., *The Study of the Ancient Near East in the Twenty-First Century: The William Foxwell Albright Centennial Conference* (Winona Lake, 1996), pp. 177–93. [Looks at Mesopotamian literature, with special emphasis on the Gilgamesh Epic, in light of modern literary theories.]

William Moran, "Ovid's *blanda voluptas* and the Humanization of Enkidu," *Journal of Near Eastern Studies* 50 (1991) 121–27. Reprinted in John Maier, ed., *Gilgamesh: A Reader* (Wauconda, IL, 1997).

William Moran, "The Gilgamesh Epic: A Masterpiece from Ancient Mesopotamia," in Jack M. Sasson, ed., *Civilizations of the Ancient Near East* (New York, 1995), vol. 4, pp. 2327–36.

A. Leo Oppenheim, *Ancient Mesopotamia: Portrait of a Dead Civilization* (Chicago and London, 1964), second edition revised by Erica Reiner (Chicago and London, 1977).

Simo Parpola, "Assyrian Library Records," *Journal of Near Eastern Studies* 42 (1983) 1–29.

J. M. Sasson, "Gilgamesh Epic," *Anchor Bible Dictionary,* vol. 2 (New York, etc., 1992), pp. 1024–27. [A succinct summary of the story of the epic.]

Jeffrey H. Tigay, *The Evolution of the Gilgamesh Epic* (Philadelphia, 1982).

Gerald P. Verbrugghe and John M. Wickersham, *Berossos and Manetho Introduced and Translated: Native Traditions in Ancient Mesopotamia and Egypt* (Ann Arbor, 1996).

Nicola Vulpe, "Irony and Unity in the Gilgamesh Epic," *Journal of Near Eastern Studies* 53 (1994) 275–83.

Christopher B. F. Walker, "The Kouyunjik Collection of Cuneiform Texts: Formation, Problems, and Prospects," pp. 183–93 in F. M. Fales and B. J. Hickey, eds. *Austen Henry Layard tra l'Oriente e Venezia* (Rome, 1987).

ILLUSTRATIONS

The illustrations on the pages that follow represent the ancient world and have been included to establish an historical context for the epic while building a bridge to modern understanding. Among them are objects not only from the era thought to include the reign of Gilgamesh the king, but objects suggesting the evolution and synthesis of tales of Gilgamesh the mythical hero into a variety of later cultures.

The captions by Robert D. Biggs outline the background of objects that reflect aspects of literature, daily life, and religion. Figures 1 and 2 suggest the beginnings of the literary tradition. Figures 3–5 may provide insight into "a day in the life of" the ancient Mesopotamian in the cradle of civilization and a connection to the modern world of that same area where similar boats and reed huts are in use today. Figures 6–10 imply the prominence of religion in the lives of the ancients. Intricately constructed ziggurats (temple-towers) and finely crafted religious statues survive as a testament to the importance of religious activity. Finally, figures 11–18 perhaps glorify and immortalize the exploits of mythical heroes in mediums ranging from vase and vessel to architecture. A prominence and universality among cultures of the art and enjoyment of storytelling is suggested.

Figures 19–33, found among the pages of the text, are from the series of original works of art by Thom Kapheim, commissioned by the publisher and designed to tell the tale in pictures. These fifteen prints from hand-carved woodcuts reflect the heroic richness and depth of an individual's attempt to define and exceed the boundaries of the world outlined by his human and religious experience.

Photograph of a fragment of Tablet XI, the "Flood Tablet" of the
Epic of Gilgamesh, inscribed in Assyrian cuneiform characters. (figure 1)

Head of the Assyrian king Ashurbanipal, 669–627 B.C., a detail of a limestone panel.
The excavations of his library provided a major source of Mesopotamian literature,
including a good portion of the *Epic of Gilgamesh*. (figure 2)

Relief decoration on a stone trough of about 1900 B.C., depicting a traditional reed house. Dwellings constructed of such bundles of reeds are still being made and occupied in the marsh areas of southern Iraq. (figure 3)

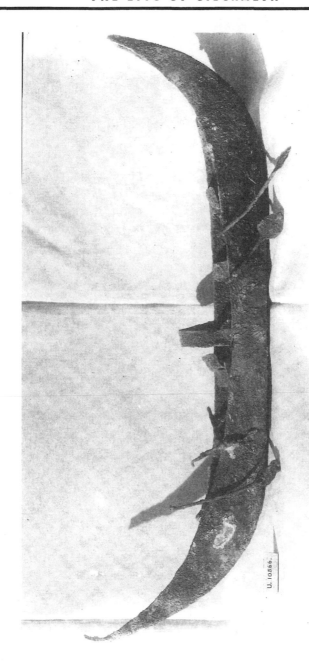

An ancient miniature boat from Ur of a type Gilgamesh might have used on his *voyage* to seek Urnapishtim. Such model boats, usually of baked clay, are often found in excavations in southern Iraq. The shape is identical to the *tarada*, the kind of boat that is even today propelled in the shallow waters of the marshes by paddles or punting poles. (figure 4)

A gypsum plaque, about 2700–2600 B.C., depicting a man and woman at a banquet, while servants bring food and drink, and musicians and dancers perform. It is believed that the hole in the center was for a peg that helped to secure doors.
(figure 5)

Ziggurat at the Eanna sanctuary at Warka, ancient Uruk, in southern Iraq. *(figure 6)*

The ziggurat at Ur during excavation in the 1930s. It was extensively restored by the Iraqi Department of Antiquities in the 1960s, but was reportedly damaged in the 1991 war. *(figure 7)*

Artist's drawing of a suggested reconstruction of the temple tower (ziggurat) of the Sumerian king Ur-Nammu, about 2100 B.C., at the ancient city of Ur. The Tower of Babel in the Bible was likely such a structure. *(figure 8)*

Copper representation of four-faced god with foot on a crouching ram and goddess holding a vase, from Ishchali, Iraq, about 18th to 17th century B.C. *(figure 9)*

Sumerian stone statuette, about 2900–2600 B.C.
Such statuettes are believed to represent a worshipper standing in a prayerful attitude
before his god in a temple. Stone was very scarce in ancient Mesopotamia, so such
statues were very expensive gifts to the deity. *(figure 10)*

Stone relief from Tell Halaf, about 1000 B.C., perhaps depicting
Gilgamesh and Enkidu's battle with Humbaba. *(figure 11)*

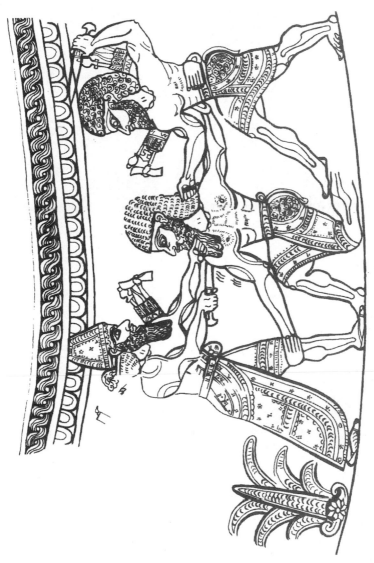

Scene engraved on an early first-millennium B.C. copper vessel (situla), perhaps Gilgamesh on the left and Enkidu on the right about to kill Humbaba. (*figure 12*)

This modern rolling of a cylinder seal in the Assyrian style of the early first millennium B.C. may depict the killing of Humbaba. *(figure 13)*

The two men attacking the figure between them, depicted on this gold bowl (in the lower right area) from Hasanlu, Iran, may represent Gilgamesh and Enkidu. *(figure 14)*

The central group in this rolling of an Assyrian seal of about 750–650 B.C. may show the monster Humbaba being attacked. *(figure 15)*

Copper double vase, each vase balanced on the head of a male wrestler, third millennium B.C. It has occasionally been suggested that such scenes represent the first meeting of Gilgamesh and Enkidu as they vie with each other. *(figure 16)*

This rolling cylinder seal of the late third millennium B.C. shows on the left a nude hero subduing a bull. It does not necessarily represent Gilgamesh attacking the Bull of Heaven, though this has been suggested. (*figure 17*)

Cylinder seal impression with hero subduing a bull, similar to the preceding one, from the third quarter of the third millenium B.C. *(figure 18)*

GILGAMESH: AN APPRECIATION¹

Gilgamesh is often considered an epic, but if so, it fails to meet all the classically mandated requirements: "An epic is a long narrative poem..."; for *Gilgamesh* is obviously much too short. But *Gilgamesh* is a poetic narrative, and it does, like the great classical epics—the *Iliad*, the *Odyssey*, and the *Aeneid*—focus on a single hero. But when we first hear of him (Tablet I), the king of Uruk doesn't seem very heroic. Whatever his past accomplishments, he now suffers a life without joy. His main current interest rests in his power to command private satisfaction, to deflower Uruk's virgin brides on their wedding nights, hoarding "the wives of other men for his own purpose" (Tablet I Column ii). This brings consternation to his people but no titillation for himself.

When it does come, the hero's conversion comes not on his own initiative, or from his own character or deeds, but, as it must have seemed to him from his own perspective, virtually by accident. Away from Uruk's Culture, out on the steppes, lives Enkidu, the hero's specially created alter ego, a shaggy wild man, a creature of Nature who communes with animals and springs their traps when they are caught. At his own father's suggestion, the hunter whose livelihood Enkidu's activities threaten petitions the king. On order of Gilgamesh, a woman named Shamhat is sent to lure Enkidu out of his primal innocence. She seduces him, tames him, makes him human. The animals of the wild now shun their former protector, "stamped[ing] away from his new self." Enkidu's bond with Nature and its "dumb beasts" is forever snapped.

Eventually Enkidu comes to town and struggles mightily with

---

1   What follows are not the reflections of a *Gilgamesh* scholar or of someone extensively versed in its secondary literature, but of someone who has often taught the work to undergraduates in literature classes. The reflections come through a triple prism: first, that of those scholars who painstakingly restored and deciphered and established an order for the *Gilgamesh* tablets; second, that of those translators who have converted *Gilgamesh* into workaday, literal English; third, that of translators like Danny Jackson who have striven to make *Gilgamesh* a work of literature in English. My aim here is not to be comprehensive, but to provoke thought and discussion.

Gilgamesh (Tablet II). The result of the struggle is an instant friendship. The king's boredom vanishes and he is now ready for action—a quest for fame. The two companions venture forth (Tablet III) to kill the giant Humbaba, guardian of the Great Cedar Forest. As they enter the forest (Tablet IV), Enkidu is wounded. They go deeper into the forest to confront Humbaba; shockingly, at the crisis point (Tablet V), it is Enkidu, himself a former guardian of Nature, who urges the killing of the pathetically pleading giant. Later, in a new venture (Tablet VI), the friends kill the Bull of Heaven, a monstrous retribution sent by the skygod Anu to humor his daughter Ishtar whose sexual advances Gilgamesh had rejected. Although once again it is apparently Gilgamesh who at Enkidu's urging delivers the *coup de grâce*, it is Enkidu's death that comes to be required as atonement for the killings of Humbaba and the Bull (Tablet VII).

Enkidu's death (Tablet VIII) plunges Gilgamesh into profoundest grief. In consequence, he undertakes a long and dangerous journey to find the secret of eternal life (Tablets IX–XI). He seeks to locate Utnapishtim, who alone with his wife had survived the Great Flood. On his harrowing journey, itself a dreamlike "liminal experience," Gilgamesh experiences the kinds of disorientation and suffering that typify rites of passage described years ago by Arnold van Gennep (*The Rites of Passage*) and more recently by Victor Turner (*The Ritual Process*). He no longer looks kinglike; he becomes worn and haggard, even frightening to behold.

On his way to Utnapishtim, Gilgamesh first meets the poison scorpions (Tablet IX): assigned to block the entrance, they soon admit Gilgamesh through the gate into the pass across the Mashu Mountains. Gilgamesh proceeds on a night journey, in pitch darkness, "blinded and frozen," arriving finally at "shorelines fresh with dew." There in a cottage lives Siduri, a Calypso-like figure (*Odyssey* Book V) "whose drinks refresh the soul." He asks her for directions, "safe passage over seas to come." She advises him, reminding him of human frailty and mortality, urging upon him the comforts and joys of temporal life, coaxing him to stay. But he goes on—to Urshanabi, the "ferryman of Utnapishtim," the Charon-like figure "who rows the seas of death." Urshanabi helps Gilgamesh across the Sea of Death (Tablet X) to the land of Utnapishtim.

On first encounter, Utnapishtim turns out to be blind, a bit crotchety, initially unhelpful, and himself rather confused on the topic of death. But he describes for Gilgamesh the events of the Great Flood (Tablet XI) and then tests his ability to withstand sleep. The hero fails, but in his failure evokes the sympathy of Utnapishtim's wife. At her suggestion, Utnapishtim rewards Gilgamesh with directions to find the plant of eternal life. Gilgamesh plucks the plant from the bottom of a lake; but on his journey back to Uruk, he bathes in a pool, leaving the plant beside the pool. A snake slithers along, filches the plant and sheds its own skin in exchange, "throwing off the past and continuing to live."[2] Gilgamesh, having lost the possibility snatched away by the snake ("now only the snake has won eternal life") but attended now by a new companion, Urshanabi, returns to Uruk, disappointed in his quest but able, it seems, to view his city with a renewed sense of accomplishment and appreciation.

The plot of *Gilgamesh*, as summarized here, and even in its fullest recoverable form, must come across at times as loose and episodic. The organic links between its parts are not always clear, yet somehow it remains a fascinating and powerful text. The fascination seems to stem from the fact that in so small a compass it offers a variety of narrative forms and types. Its power comes from its presentation of central themes of major significance.

To illustrate, I begin by confessing that when years ago I first read *Gilgamesh*, the initial encounter between Gilgamesh and Enkidu ("So the mighty brothers fought at first / pushing and shoving each other / for hours and hours enraged"—Tablet II Column vi) reminded me of some boyhood television watching: the Disney series on Davy Crockett, particularly the episode when Davy meets up with the riverboatman Mike Fink. In my recollection, a ferocious battle takes place; Davy whups Mike; the foes become friends. The Forest King and the River King join hands to advance the American frontier. Years later, in thumbing through the life of Lincoln by his former law partner, William Herndon—a mix of fact and legend—I found that young Abe had once wrassled a local tough named Jack Armstrong, the match leading in its conclusion to a lifelong friendship—or so says Billy Herndon.

This is the stuff of entertaining tall tales; *Gilgamesh*, of course, is far more than that. At a nobler end of the spectrum of narrative forms it calls

---

2   For the snake's symbolic aspects: Joseph Campbell, *The Power of Myth* 45–47 (quote, p. 45).

to mind Mircea Eliade's definition of myths as always and everywhere sacred stories of creation, set in the timeless time of the beginnings, provably true because they are validated by present experience.[3] *Gilgamesh* is mythic in this sense in many of its features, but especially in two episodes that embrace the story's core: near the beginning, Enkidu's loss of innocence through carnal seduction, and toward the end, Gilgamesh's loss to the snake of the plant of eternal life. The complex of man, woman, serpent, and plant, although widely separated and much attenuated in *Gilgamesh*, nevertheless calls to mind the similar complex in Genesis 2:4–3:24,[4] where, in the interpretation that is most persuasive from a mythic standpoint, the knowledge Adam and Eve gain by eating the "fruit" offered by the serpent is carnal knowledge:[5] in exchange for godlike knowledge and its attendant loss of innocence, a loss of physical immortality but acquisition of an access to another kind of immortality, the ability to procreate future generations. Neither Gilgamesh nor Enkidu acts upon the possibility, but it is symbolically present through much of the story and is greatly emphasized in Siduri's advice to Gilgamesh (Tablet X Column iii): "Cherish children to whom your love gives life…. Play joyfully with your chosen wife."[6]

Similarly mythic and shared with Genesis is *Gilgamesh*'s early identification and concern for the ever tense relationship between Nature and Culture, "one of the central and most universal preoccupations of speculative myths."[7] This relationship, a favorite of structuralist interpretation, has just been alluded to in reference to the episode of Enkidu's taming. There, a representative of extreme Nature, Enkidu, is tamed by a female representative of extreme urban Culture.[8] The clash

3   The definition is presented in slightly different wordings in various places. Here I rely on *Myth and Reality* 5–8.
4   Campbell, *The Power of Myth* 45–50.
5   W. Gunther Plaut (ed.), *The Torah: A Modern Commentary* 38–42, at 39.
6   See further David Halperin, *One Hundred Years of Homosexuality* 75–87, especially 81.
7   G. S. Kirk, *Myth: Its Meaning and Functions*, esp. 132–152 (quote, p. 132), mostly on Gilgamesh and Enkidu; also excellent as a summary and discussion of the story as a whole, especially careful to distinguish between its Sumerian and its Akkadian versions. See further Thomas Van Nortwick, *Somewhere I Have Never Travelled* 8–38.
8   Although the woman is nowhere stated to be a prostitute, much less a "temple" or

between Nature and Culture, however, is just as apparent in the Humbaba episode. On one level, the episode is a simple heroic exploit, though clearly, as Enkidu and Ninsun, Gilgamesh's mother, and all the people of Uruk feared, loaded with special danger. If the episode is read merely as an exploit, Humbaba becomes the brawny, scary, villainous ogre of folktale; but in another reading—one stressed by the storyteller—Humbaba is the divinely appointed Guardian of the Sacred Cedar Forest: "Enlil it was who sent Humbaba there/to scare away intruders with fierce/and frightening howls." His killing marks the beginning of the inexorable end of the forest he was ordained to protect.[9] When he falls, like Old Ben in William Faulkner's "The Bear," "—the old bear, solitary, indomitable, and alone—," the forest is "doomed." What was once sacred is profaned. Nature succumbs to Culture. One can hear the axes beginning to chop away at Humbaba's great cedars, and the shrieking of the logging train ("It had been harmless once....It had been harmless then.") that will destroy Old Ben's Wilderness.[10]

Besides big themes like "Loss of Innocence" and "Nature and Culture," there are other, quite specific Biblical parallels.[11] Two are prominent. The less familiar is found in Tablet VI, where the dealings of Ishtar, Gilgamesh, and Ishtar's father, Anu, amount to a variant of the Potiphar's wife motif, so called from the story of Joseph in Genesis Chapter 39.[12] In this motif, an aggressive older woman attempts the virtue of the story's hero. Rebuffed and therefore vindictive, she seeks revenge by charging the hero with improper conduct, usually (but not in *Gilgamesh*) attempted rape. The charges, usually made to her husband or father, are believed, and he then threatens or destroys the hero's well-being. The motif has been popular in many story traditions, perhaps because it mirrors or, in a technical sense,

---

"sacred" prostitute, this has often been assumed. The Mesopotamian sensibilities about this institution no doubt strike us as alien, as they did Herodotus (1.199) two thousand five hundred years ago.

9   John Perlin, *A Forest Journey* 35–43.

10 For further thoughts on sacred forests, and the impact of Culture on Nature, see Simon Schama, *Landscape and Memory*, especially Part One, and in Part One, especially Chapter 4 (the profanation followed by the sacralizing of the giant sequoias of California).

11 Alexander Heidel, *The Gilgamesh Epic and Old Testament Parallels*, Chapter IV (224–269).

12 Shalom Goldman (*The Wiles of Women, the Wiles of Men*) notes the presence of the Potiphar's wife motif in *Gilgamesh* (43–44, 80), but does not discuss it at length.

"projects" the concerns of the Oedipus complex. In the complex, the "son" pursues the "mother" and wants to eliminate the "father"; in the motif, the "son" rejects the pursuing "mother" and risks being destroyed by his "father." The prevalence of the motif, like the Oedipus complex and its associated myths, darkly hints at recurring familial and human problems. There are various ancient examples—the Egyptian "Tale of the Two Brothers," the Greek legends of Bellerophon (*Iliad* VI.144–211) and of Hippolytus, especially in the Euripidean tragedy by that name;[13] but there are also many modern reworkings, including Harper Lee's *To Kill a Mockingbird* (still on many high school reading lists); Bernard Malamud's *The Fixer;* and, above all, Richard Wright's great and terrifying novel, *Native Son.*

But far better known than the Potiphar's wife motif in *Gilgamesh,* and causing a great stir when it first became known, is the story of the flood as recounted by Utnapishtim in Tablet XI. Its match with the Noah flood story in Genesis 6–8 was startling. From the building of their "arks" to their manifold release of birds to determine that their respective floods had subsided, the two stories contain parallels that can hardly be coincidental. But differences of perspective may in the end be far more impressive than the similarities of narrative detail. After Noah survived, for example, he gave sacrificial thanks and went about his business, increasing and multiplying;[14] but when Utnapishtim saw the carnage left by the deluge, the first thing he did was weep:

> Then I see a dawn so still;
> all humans beaten to dirt
> and earth itself like some vast roof.
> I peeked through the portal into a morning sun
> then turned, knelt and cried.
> Tears flooded down my face.

(Tablet XI Column iii)

---

13 Where Hippolytus' vicious and misogynistic rejection of his stepmother Phaedra's desires seems to reflect the curses Gilgamesh rains down on Ishtar—a catalogue of her former unfortunate sex partners. For another such catalogue, but conceived and told in rollicking good humor, see *Iliad* XIV ("The Deception of Zeus" by his wife Hera: Zeus, overcome with passion for Hera, insensitively lists, lines 312–328, his former partners). The Bull of Heaven in *Gilgamesh* seems to prefigure the bull summoned by Theseus to destroy his son Hippolytus.

14 Elie Wiesel, *Sages and Dreamers* 19–34.

The remorseful Mesopotamian gods regret their flood ("Even Ishtar then bemoaned the/fates of her sad people") and squabble: "[H]ow dare you drown so many little people / without consulting me?" says Ea to Enlil (Column iv). "Why not just kill the one who offended you, / drown only the guilty?" The Biblical God has no such second thoughts, no regrets, and no one to question His decisions.

Even Alexander Heidel, who devoted so much effort to reclaim *Gilgamesh* for a wide modern audience, found the Genesis flood account both beyond question and morally superior to the one in *Gilgamesh*. The flood in *Gilgamesh*, for Heidel, has almost no "moral or ethical motive." The flood itself is capricious, the polytheistic gods are silly, cowardly, and confused. The Biblical flood, however, "is sent by the one omnipotent God, who is just in all his dealings with the children of men, who punishes the impenitent sinner, even if it means the destruction of the world, but who saves the just with his powerful hand and in his own way." The Genesis deluge is "clearly and unmistakably a moral judgment....Although God resolves not to send another flood, he is nowhere represented as *regretting* the diluvial catastrophe."[15] The absence of regret is (supposedly) commendable.

With all due respect to Heidel (and the respect is considerable), it may be preferable to approach the two flood stories with another sensibility: that is, to view Heidel's reading of the Biblical account as presenting the world as we desperately want it to be: stable (once the flood is over), just and predictable, in Someone's reliable control; the Mesopotamian account as presenting the world as we often experience it, with its messy contingencies and all-too-common horrors. Such an approach, of course, can provoke some very disturbing questions, most especially: What about the children who (logically) must also have been overwhelmed by the deluge, "those who never could inscribe themselves in the Book of Life with deeds either good or evil, great or small, because their lives were cut off before they had their chance?"[16]

Obviously *Gilgamesh* does not fear to raise such questions—and others

---

15 Heidel, *The Gilgamesh Epic* 268–269 (Heidel's emphasis).

16 Hans Jonas, "The Concept of God after Auschwitz," in Albert H. Friedlander (ed.), *Out of the Whirlwind: A Reader of Holocaust Literature* 465–476 (quote, 474–475). See also Fyodor Dostoyevsky, *The Brothers Karamazov*, Book 5, Chapter 4 ("Rebellion") and Claude Lanzmann, *Shoah*, especially 188–190 (on Adam Czerniakow's suicide and its motive).

besides. It is throughout concerned with the issues of heroism and friendship, death and grief, and these are what often draw readers to its pages. In terms presented by Ernest Becker in his *Denial of Death*, a powerful blend of Kierkegaard's existentialism and Otto Rank's psychology, Gilgamesh's exploits with Enkidu should probably be viewed as defenses that keep the hero from pondering his own mortality and save him from the madness that such pointblank reflection must cause. When his exploits are over and his friend has died, he must look into his own abyss and face the madness. That first experience of a loved one's death, that explosion of mental dissociation, the numbing shock that cannot block the ripping, howling agony that many of us have felt, is an archetypal, universal event, and Gilgamesh's experience of it is every bit as emotionally overwhelming as Achilles' when he receives word of Patroklos' death in *Iliad* XVIII:

> In both hands he caught up the grimy dust, and poured it
> over his head and face, and fouled his handsome countenance,
> and the black ashes were scattered over his immortal tunic.
> And he himself, mightily in his might, in the dust lay
> at length, and took and tore at his hair with his hands,
> and defiled it.
>
> (lines 23–27, Richmond Lattimore translation)

Like Achilles, Gilgamesh feels the guilt of a survivor somehow responsible for his friend's death, "my friend who was always there for me." And his friend's death threatens to break "the survivor's life into unhealable halves, with everything before his death radically severed from everything after."[17]

Pace Wittgenstein ("For life in the present there is no death. Death is not an event in life. It is not a fact of the world."),[18] Enkidu's death proves to Gilgamesh that, when all is said and done, death is after all "an event in life" that must be "lived through" and understood.[19] His great journey begins with a concern for Enkidu's life but shifts in its course to a concern for his own life—and death. So he grieves first for Enkidu, suffering those stages identified nearly thirty years ago by Elisabeth Kübler-Ross *(On Death and Dying)*, especially the rage and the depression and the bargaining; but

---

17 Jonathan Shay, *Achilles in Vietnam* 39–40.
18 From Wittgenstein's Notebooks 1914–1916 as excerpted in Jonathan Westphal and Carl Levenson, eds., *Life and Death* 147.
19 John S. Dunne, *Time and Myth*, especially 7–15.

he grieves also for himself. In mid-journey he tells Urshanabi:

> I can't stop pacing. I can't stop crying.
> My friend has died and half my heart
>   is torn from me.
> Won't I soon be like him, stone-cold and dead
>   for all the days to come?

(Tablet X Column iii)

But at the end, when his journey is over, when at the story's closing he begins—but only begins—to describe Uruk for Urshanabi ("Rise up now, Urshanabi, and examine Uruk's wall . . ."), he seems to have accepted both Enkidu's loss and his own mortality. In the meantime, Gilgamesh's life goes on and we learn from his example. For we have just closed the pages of a work that reminds us

> that a compelling narrative, offering a storyteller's moral
> imagination vigorously at work, can enable any of us to learn
> by example, to take to heart what is, really, a gift of grace.[20]

James G. Keenan
Loyola University of Chicago

---

20 Robert Coles, *The Call of Stories* 191.

Secondary Works Cited

Becker, Ernest. *The Denial of Death*. The Free Press: New York, 1973.

Campbell, Joseph. *The Power of Myth*. Doubleday: New York, 1988 (with Bill Moyers).

Coles, Robert. *The Call of Stories: Teaching and the Moral Imagination*. Houghton Mifflin Company: Boston, 1989.

Dunne, John S. *Time and Myth: A Meditation on Storytelling as an Exploration of Life and Death*. University of Notre Dame Press: Notre Dame and London, 1975.

Eliade, Mircea. *Myth and Reality*. Harper Torchbooks: New York, 1963.

Goldman, Shalom. *The Wiles of Women, the Wiles of Men: Joseph and Potiphar's Wife in Ancient Near Eastern, Jewish, and Islamic Folklore*. State University of New York Press: Albany, 1995.

Halperin, David. *One Hundred Years of Homosexuality and Other Essays on Greek Love* (Chapter 4, "Heroes and Their Pals," 75–87). Routledge, Chapman and Hall, Inc.: New York and London, 1990.

Heidel, Alexander. *The Gilgamesh Epic and Old Testament Parallels*. The University of Chicago Press: Chicago and London, reprint 1963; original publication 1946.

Jonas, Hans. "The Concept of God after Auschwitz," in Albert H. Friedlander (ed.), *Out of the Whirlwind: A Reader of Holocaust Literature*. Schocken Books: New York, 1976 (pp. 465– 476).

Kirk, G. S. *Myth: Its Meaning and Functions in Ancient and Other Cultures*. The University of California Press: Berkeley and Los Angeles, 1970.

Kübler-Ross, Elisabeth. *On Death and Dying*. Macmillan Publishing Company: New York, 1969.

Lanzmann, Claude. *Shoah: An Oral History of the Holocaust*. Pantheon Books: New York, 1985.

Perlin, John. *A Forest Journey: The Role of Wood in the Development of Civilization.* Harvard University Press: Cambridge, MA, and London, 1991.

Plaut, W. Gunther, ed. *The Torah: A Modern Commentary.* The Union of American Hebrew Congregations: New York, 1981.

Schama, Simon. *Landscape and Memory.* Alfred A. Knopf: New York, 1995.

Shay, Jonathan. *Achilles in Vietnam: Combat Trauma and the Undoing of Character.* Atheneum: New York, 1994.

Turner, Victor. *The Ritual Process: Structure and Anti-Structure.* Aldine Publishing Company: Chicago, 1969.

Van Gennep, Arnold. *The Rites of Passage.* The University of Chicago Press: Chicago, 1960 (reissue of the 1909 English translation by Monika B. Vizedom and Gabrielle T. Caffee).

Van Nortwick, Thomas. *Somewhere I Have Never Travelled: The Hero's Journey* (Chapter 1, "The Wild Man: *The Epic of Gilgamesh*," 3–38). Oxford University Press: New York and Oxford, 1996.

Westphal, Jonathan, and Levenson, Carl, eds. *Life and Death.* Hackett Readings in Philosophy. Hackett Publishing Company: Indianapolis and Cambridge, 1993.

Wiesel, Elie. *Sages amd Dreamers: Biblical, Talmudic and Hasidic Portraits and Legends* ("Noah," 9–34). Summit Books: New York, 1991.

My Poetic Intention

MY POETIC INTENTION

Translation as Compromise

When dealing with this epic's linguistic and aesthetic controversies, the best we can do is to admit humbly that we do not have answers now to seminal questions about this text. The tentativeness of my position is directly related to what I believe is a reality of modern academic life. There is no high school or undergraduate course sequence in the English speaking countries for training translators of cuneiform.

My training is as a comparative classicist. I've had fifteen years of instruction in Greek and Latin, half as many in French and Spanish. Luck had me grow up hearing several dialects as "natural tongues." My knowledge of cuneiform is self-taught and cursory, but I've written poetry in English almost daily for thirty years. Like Ezra Pound, I believe a translator's success has to do with poetic grace, balance, finesse, sleight of hand, and luck.

What is often said about the politics and prejudices of translators is true. But it should by now be obvious that since all translation is a compromise one should hardly be criticized severely for agreeing to take part in what, by its nature, is an act of reconciling one precise word for another.

Influences on My *Gilgamesh*

My acquaintance with the original *Gilgamesh* text was limited to visits I made to the University of Pennsylvania Museum of Archaeology where the late Father Hermann Behrens and Earl Leichty were kind enough to read for me from the fragmented tablets shepherded in their collection. I was aware of only seven English editions of the poem as I began my work in November of 1991. These were by Thompson (1928), Leonard (1934), Heidel (1946), Mason (1970), Sandars (1972), Maier/Gardner (1984), and Kovacs (1989). From these I absorbed theories, exempla, advice, energy, tips, mistakes, images, and a sense of comradeship that let me find my own place in their century-long effort to scale what someone might compare to a peak like Everest. Their failures informed me. Their successes challenged me. Their inability to produce a definitive final word on our task left me knowing that I would also fail to create a "perfect" rendition...no matter how long I tried...no matter how hard I worked. Whatever else it's been, this endeavor has been a lesson in humility.

Several teachers prior to those efforts taught me how to endure the Herculean labors of epic translation. I studied with Bernard Dick, Allen Mandlebaum, and Frederick Golden in New York City and taught with James Mantiband at Brooklyn College. Their work on the *Aeneid,* the *Divine Comedy,* and the *Song of Roland* shaped my tastes.

Ezra Pound's experiments, especially his "Homage To Sextus Propertius," have meant more to me than those of others who've failed to see how art delights in its ineffable beauty, while they've slavishly pursued a truth that intimidates more than it thrills.

On a very tangential note, an article by Ehud Ya'ari and Ina Friedman, "Curses in Verses" (*Atlantic Monthly,* February 1991), also influenced me. Rhyme schemes at certain parts of the text (Tablet VI, lines 35ff.) owe something to the Near Eastern tradition of mock-poetry.

Another influence may be found in Tablet XII, line 12, where Gilgamesh advises Enkidu, who is preparing to visit the underworld,[1] on matters of protocol. I sought a song with a similar message, whose rhythm I could use to cloak the words of this section, so that it would resonate with reverence appropriate for an approach to the spirits of the dead. I chose one of Western music's most ancient hymns ("Oh Come, Oh Come, Emmanuel"). If the reader can keep the tune in mind without thinking of a Catholic Mass, the passage achieves the pace and solemnity I hoped to afford.

I'd prefer to think that Sin-leqe-unninni, the scholar-scribe widely believed to be the editor or compiler of the so-called "Standard Version" of *Gilgamesh,* would favor such word play. Such innovations raise the stakes for later translators who will either ignore the challenge or imitate patterns of language that energize the story.

---

1 An excellent new contribution to the literature of underworld journeys appeared in 1996. It is Alan Epstein's *The Formations of Hell,* Cornell University Press.

Translation as Choice

A very specific controversy among translators of Gilgamesh centers on how *harimtu* or *šamhatu*, words associated with Shamhat, should be rendered. "Harlot" and "courtesan" appear in certain versions (Ferry, 1992, and Gardner/Maier, 1984). Others use the word "priestess" (Leonard, 1934). Some are quaint (Spenser calls her "lass" in a 1958 translation); others try to be neutral (Mason says "a creature"). I chose to use a number of options ("sacred temple priestess," "dispenser of Ishtar's sacrament," "lover," "woman,") for several reasons.

As I said in the introduction to the first edition, we can't fully understand or appreciate the role of temple attendants in ancient sexual cults. To condemn their behavior with modern standards is misleading, especially since prostitution was not practiced then in the way it is today in the streets of our cities. I met many streetwalkers in the summer of 1985 while researching an article on teenage prostitution for the *New York Times*. None of the young women I interviewed reminded me at all of Shamhat as a character in *Gilgamesh*. Her èlan and the civilizing effect she has on Enkidu are too complicated to be reduced to a one-word description. "Wife" clearly won't do. So I selected what I hope are non-judgmental terms in order to avoid perpetuating what I see as mistakes.

It is edifying to note how one single line in Tablet I, Column iv has been translated or altered by various writers.

The original reads:

> *ur-tam-mi* ^sal *Šam-hat di-da-ša ur-ša ip-te-e-ma ku-zu-ub-ša il-qí*

I translate this to mean:

> *Shamhat let her garments loose and spread forth her happiness.*

Gardner/Maier renders it:

> *The courtesan untied her wide belt and spread her legs.*

Which is more graphic? And how do they compare to Leonard, who writes:

> *The priestess loosened her buckle and unveiled her delight.*

Does the translator's gender seem to matter? Consider the

translation of Nancy Sandars:

She was not ashamed to take him, she made herself naked and welcomed his eagerness.

...or of Maureen Kovacs:

Shamhat unclutched her bosom, exposed her sex and he took in her voluptuousness.

Mason paraphrases the whole passage while calling her a prostitute.

Speiser says:

The lass freed her breasts, bared her bosom and he possessed her ripeness.

In 1987 Foster claimed she:

Unloosed her attire and opened her vulva.

And in two versions from 1992, translators return to the extremes when Ferry sounds Victorian while resurrecting "harlot" to describe Shamhat, and Zeman makes her sound like Snow White in Disneyland (without actually mentioning whatever she did).

Maybe Heidel has had the last laugh on us all. In 1946 he wisely sidestepped this entire brouhaha by rendering this section, which Smith's 1876 version omits, into Latin!

Meretrix nudabat sinum suum, aperiebat gremium suum....

I can't say briefly how all this seems to me. Students everywhere can now fight among themselves fully confident that the descendants of the Tower of Babel are alive and well!

Translation as an Equation

Equations fascinate students of math. Those interested in literature rarely devise such formulas, but they routinely suspect that poetic complexities might be reduced to simplicities like the ones enjoyed by their classmates in arithmetic. If someone forced me to create an algebraic equivalent for my rendition of *Gilgamesh*, the best I could offer would be this:

$$\text{original text}^5 + \text{Smith} - \text{Thompson x Heidel}^2 + \frac{\text{Mason}}{\text{Sandars}} \times \text{Maier}^4 - \text{Kovacs} = \text{Jackson}$$

Meaning what?

Meaning this: The original text, even in its fragmentary form, remains the start for all versions, but the earliest English translations become a great part of each new translator's opus. I would not omit Smith or Heidel from this explanation because I deeply appreciate the prototypic work they struggled to create while not trying to be as populist as my publisher encouraged me to be. But I owe more to John Maier (with whom I studied after producing my rendition) than to those I found prosaic, unpoetic, or wooden.

In the final effort, of course, we each err in our own way. For this second edition, I refashioned sections that now reflect a growing appreciation I have for a task that perhaps deserves more respect than I possessed five years ago. In a few lines I have used language less likely to offend. Other sections have been fine-tuned in a way that our first deadlines would not permit. Consequently, there's an improvement. And I remain convinced that the Bolchazy-Carducci edition is still the most valuable *Gilgamesh* available to teachers.

Translations in History

As a comparatist by training, my approach to Babylonian literature is flavored by my regard for other ancient texts and translations. To explain how I regard the Twentieth Century's efforts to bring *Gilgamesh* to America's students, I would have to refer to well-documented comparable efforts in related fields. I do this because I am convinced that Maier and Kovacs and Ferry and I are part of a continuum, one that has room for others and which will endure long after we're gone.

This is certainly how other epics challenged earlier translators. The Vergilian efforts of Gavin Douglass, John Dryden, Joseph Addison, and William Wordsworth preceded those of C. Day Lewis, Robert Fitzgerald, and Seamus Heaney. Each worked the *Aeneid's* sections differently because of the time, tone, politics, rhyme, and capacities of an age. Each chose a music to promote or ignore. Each knew the original and knew when to disregard the original while paying attention to earlier translations or to the previously unscripted hymns that fill a translator's ears late at night when echoes of ancient traditions seem clearest, loudest, or most beautiful.

Because of their sensitivity to language's inexhaustible potential for newness, these poets rendered versions of Vergil that tested their talents while allowing them to present productions of a story to thrill, sadden, edify, and amuse readers who would not have known the *Aeneid* without them.

So it is with *Gilgamesh.* The ten-or-so English versions in our century testify to an increasing fascination and determination on the part of scholars, schools, and publishers to invest the future with a strong sense of the past. And it is refreshing for me to be a part of a movement that has worked carefully to investigate a part of antiquity ignored for so, so long.

Gilgamesh's Future

Since the shelf life of even good poetry is often only a decade or so, it isn't likely that others will wait long to add even newer contributions to the list of this epic's translators. Some will borrow Gardner/Maier's depth or Sandar's fluency or Kovacs' exactness. Others may be misled by my poetic liberties or by the liberties taken by Ferry as he rendered the verse into couplets foreign to the original. A few may embellish *Gilgamesh* with poetry that is today unimaginable. It becomes increasingly less likely that anyone will be able to start from scratch because so much has already been done and the growing number of English translations will likely inform future attempts to render the epic in one way or another.

In America's classrooms today sit students with greater diversity than ever before. Because their multiculturalism has modified the emphasis and direction of classical studies, the future of their own place in *Gilgamesh's* history seems promising. It is likely that Achilles or Aeneas will remain central to Western thought. But it is just as likely now that Enkidu and his remarkable friend will replace others in the pantheon of characters whose stories shape the thoughts of students. I relish the possibility that fifty years from now my poetry may imbue some young person with an interest in antiquity or amuse some reader for a few hours by taking an imaginative, historical leap into so distant and so relevant a world.

Danny P. Jackson

ACKNOWLEDGMENTS

I wish to thank those who taught me to render the thought as well as the word while introducing me to various languages at Manhattan's Cathedral Seminary, Iona, Forham, Columbia, and the City University of New York. My students, especially Dennis Gonya, Andrea Santo, Jacquie Battle, Carl Hoffman, and Susan Fries, as well as my own children, Dan and Cara, and my wife Lorraine have guided my hand in yet another way. Special tribute is due to my parents and siblings, not only for teaching me to read, but for having been the gentlest of Irish storytellers.

I would also like hereby to acknowledge several unlikely debts:
- to the ancient Celts, especially Boudicca
- to those who've loved me truly
- to the moons and stars I've seen in dreams above Slieve Gullion Mountain in Ireland
- to the children of the Bronx
- to those who've paved my way, especially Lou Bolchazy and Marie Carducci
- to the Sisters of Mercy at Georgian Court College in Lakewood, New Jersey
- to the memories of Dorothy Day and Bobby Sands
- *amatis morte in adolescentia afflictis animaeque femineae semper amandae*
- and I especially acknowledge my heartfelt thanks to the Christian God who filled my youth with joy

Danny P. Jackson
Point Pleasant Beach, New Jersey
Christmas, 1996

Main Characters of the Epic

Gilgamesh, the hero and king of Uruk

Enkidu, his new friend

Ninsun, wise goddess and mother of Gilgamesh

Shamhat, sacred priestess who brought the two friends together

Anu, father of the gods and patron of Uruk

Humbaba, monster god who must be killed

Ishtar, the king's spurned and vengeful suitor-goddess

Enlil, god who unleashes the great flood

Siduri, the barmaid with worldly advice

Urshanabi, the boatman who gives passage to paradise

Utnapishtim, who holds the secret of eternal life

who hoards the wives of other men for his own purpose
(figure 19)

Tablet I
Columns i – vi

Gilgamesh, the King

The Creation of Enkidu

The Civilization of Enkidu

Gilgamesh Dreams of Enkidu

Column i

Fame haunts the man who visits hell,
who lives to tell my entire tale identically.
So like a sage, a trickster or saint,
GILGAMESH —wisdom
was a hero who knew secrets and saw forbidden places,
who could even speak of the time before the
Flood because he lived long, learned much,
and spoke his life to those who first
cut into clay his bird-like words.

10   He commanded walls for Uruk and for Eanna,
our holy ground,
walls that you can see still; walls where weep
the weary widows of dead soldiers.
Go to them and touch their immovable presence
with gentle finger to find yourself.
No one else ever built such walls.
Climb Uruk's Tower and walk about on a
windy night. Look. Touch. Taste. Sense.
What force creates such mass?

20   Open up the special box that's hidden in the wall
and read aloud the story of Gilgamesh's life.
Learn what sorrow taught him; learn of those
he overcame by wit or force or fear as he,
a town's best child, acted nobly in the way
one should to lead and acted wisely too
as one who sought no fame.
Child of Lugalbanda's wife and some great force,
Gilgamesh is a fate alive, the
finest babe of Ninsun, she who never

30   let a man touch her, indeed
so pure and heavenly, so without fault.
He knew the secret paths that reached the eagle's
nest above the mountain and he knew too how

just to drop a well into the chilly earth.
He sailed the sea to where Shamash comes,
explored the world, sought life, and came at last
to Utnapishtim far away who did bring
back to life the flooded earth. → *Seeks the secret of eternal life.*
Is there anywhere a greater king

40 who can say, as Gilgamesh may,
"I am supreme"?
↳ *Superior figure*

Column ii → *demigod*

The bigger part of him was made in heaven
and the smaller part somewhere on earth.
She, Ninsun, fashioned his body's self.
She endowed him.
Gilgamesh watches the flocks of Uruk himself
as if he were a loose bull, nose up in open field.
Gilgamesh's tribe is invincible→ *powerful but not perfect*
and is aroused by small insults.

50 He himself howls
through sacred places
where his sacrilege is hidden → *hidden sins (abuser of power/*
from the view of youngsters. *image)*
"Is this the shepherd of Uruk's flocks,
our strength, our light, our reason,
who hoards the wives of other men → *womanizer*
for his own purpose?"
A prayer of opposition rose from Uruk's other men to heaven;
and the attentive gods asked:
"Who created this awesome beast

60 with an unmatched strength and a
chant that fosters armies?
This warrior keeps boys from fathers – *splitting of families*
in the night and in the day.
Is this Gilgamesh,
is this the shepherd of Uruk's flocks,

our strength, our light, our reason,
who hoards the wives of other men
for his own purpose?"
When Anu in the sky heard this,

70   he said to Aruru, great goddess of creation that she is:
"You created humans; create again in the
image of Gilgamesh and let this imitation be
as quick in heart and as strong in arm
so that these counterforces might first engage,
then disengage, and finally let Uruk's children
live in peace."
Hearing that, Aruru thought of Anu. Then she
wet her creative fingers, fashioned a rock, and tossed
it as far as she could into the woods.

80   Thus she fathered Enkidu, a forester, and gave birth
in terror and in fright without a single cry of pain,
bringing forth another likeness of Ninurta, god of war.
Hair covered his body and his curls resembled
those of any daughter, growing swiftly like the
fair hair of Nisaba-giver-of-grain.
This Enkidu had neither clan nor race. He went
clothed as one who shepherds well, eating the food
of grass, drinking from the watery holes of herds
and racing swift as wind or silent water.

90   Then Enkidu met a hunter at the watery hole
on three consecutive days.
And each time the face of the hunter signaled
recognition of Enkidu.
For the herds were uninvited at
the hunter's oasis and the hunter was
disturbed by this intrusion. His quiet heart
rushed up in trouble. His eyes darkened.
Fear leaped forth onto a face that looks
as if it expects to doubt for a long, long time.

His strength is like Anu's swift star, and
tirelessly does he roam across the land...
like the beasts
(figure 20)

Column iii

100 Then with trembling lips the hunter told his father
     this complaint:
"Sir, one has come to my watery hole from afar and he
is the biggest and best throughout the land. He feels power.
His is a strength like that of Anu's swift star, and
tirelessly does he roam across the land.
He eats the food of beasts and, like the beasts,
he comes at will to drink from my watery hole.
In fear do I see him come to undo
what I have done by wrecking traps, by
bursting mounds, by letting animals slip through my
110 grasp, beasts that I would bind."
Then with hateful lips, the father told the hunter his reply:
"Boy, your answer lies in Uruk where
there stalks a man of endless strength named Gilgamesh.
He is the biggest and best throughout the land. He feels power.
His is a strength like that of Anu's swift star.
Start out toward Uruk's ancient palace
and tell your tale to Gilgamesh.
In turn he'll say to set a trap, take back with
you a fine lover, some sacred temple priestess,
120 who might let him see what force and charm a woman has.
Then as Enkidu comes again to the watery hole
let her strip in nearby isolation to show him all her grace.
If he is drawn toward her, and leaves the herd to mate,
his beasts on high will leave him then behind."
The hunter heard his father well and went that very night
to Uruk where he said this to Gilgamesh:
"There is someone from afar whose
force is great throughout our land.
130 His is a strength throughout the land. He feels power.
His is a strength like that of Anu's swift star, and
tirelessly does he roam across the land.
He eats the food of beasts and, like the beasts,

he comes at will to drink from my watery hole.
In fear do I see him come to undo
what I have done by wrecking traps, by
bursting mounds, by letting animals slip through my
grasp, beasts that I would bind."
So Gilgamesh replied:
"Go set a trap; take back with *fear of overpower by &*
140 you a fine lover, Shamhat, the sacred temple priestess, *love trap*
who might let him see what charm and force a woman has.
Then as Enkidu comes again to the watery hole,
let her strip in nearby isolation to show him all her grace.
If he is drawn toward her, and leaves the herd to mate,
his beasts on high will leave him then behind."
The hunter returned, bringing with him the dispenser
     of Ishtar's sacrament,
and swift was their journey.
Three days later, at the watery hole, they set their
trap for Enkidu and spoke no word for two
150 whole days waiting and waiting and waiting.
Then the herd came slowly in to drink.

Column iv

Beasts arose and sleepy limbs began to flutter then.
Enkidu, the boy who walked on mountains,
who eats the food of beasts and, like the beasts,
comes down at will to drink from the watery hole,
with the beasts arose and stretched
his tired limbs to start the day.
She beheld him then, as he was in his beginning,
the one who gave and took life from the far woods.
160 "Here is he, fine lover; be set to wet him with
your tongue and chest and loins.
Spread forth your happiness. Display your hidden charm.
Jump him fast and kneel upon his shoulders.
Without his wind then, he'll enter near your entrance.

let her strip in nearby isolation to show him all her grace.
If he is drawn toward her and leaves the herd to mate,
his beasts on high will leave him then behind.
(figure 21)

Take off your robe to let him in.
Let him see what force a woman has.
The friends he has from on wild will exile him
if he presses his person, as he will, into your scented bush."
Shamhat let her garments loose and spread forth
170 her happiness, which Enkidu entered as a wind god
enters an open cavern's mouth. → *fascinate d*
                                      with her
Hot and swollen first, she jumped him fast
knocking out his rapid breath with
thrust after loving thrust.
She let him see what force a woman has,
and he stayed within her scented bush for
seven nights, leaping, seeping, weeping, and sleeping there.
After that week of pleasure,
Enkidu returned to the herds
180 but the beasts fled from him in haste.
They stampeded away from his new self.
He could no longer race as he had once,
legs soft now and ankles stiff. The beasts
left him behind and he grew sad
that he could no longer speed with them.
But he enjoyed the memory that no virgin has
and, returning to his fine lover, he once
more knelt between her legs
as she spoke these words to him:
190 "Now you are as if a god,
with no more need of dumb beasts, however fair.
We can now ascend the road to Uruk's palace,
the immaculate domicile, where Anu and Ishtar dwell,
and there we will see Gilgamesh, the powerful,
who rides over the herd like any great king."
These words he heard and he stared at her.
For the first time he wished for just one friend.
Then Enkidu asked the love who was so fine:
"Please come with me and be my love
200 at the immaculate domicile, where Anu and Ishtar dwell,

and there we will see Gilgamesh, the powerful,
who rides over the herd like any great king.
I wish to call on him; to proclaim all things
aloud and find a friend in him."

Column v

Enkidu continued:
"Uruk will hear me say, 'I am the strongest.
I alone can do all I wish.'
Forester that I am, a mountainous power is mine.
We should march together, face-by-face,
210 so I can promote your fame."
Then fine lover said these words in invitation:
"Enter Uruk of the herds, Enkidu,
where costumes bright are worn,
where it is always time to party,
where merry music never fades,
where graceful girls do ever play
with toys and boys and men;
for in the night these revelers do
their best to rule the town.
220 There, with a smile, Enkidu
will see his other self, great Gilgamesh.
Watch him all, please. Note his
face, his fists, his fairest sword,
and all the strength that dwells in him.
Could he be greater than you,
this one who's up and down all day and night?
Fear your own anger; for great Gilgamesh
adores fair Shamash and is adored in turn.
Anu of the blue sky, Enlil from the clouds
230 and clever Ea have empowered him.
And before he even sees you,
this great Gilgamesh will have first envisioned you
in Uruk as a rival in a dream."

Gilgamesh awakens to ask his mother, Ninsun,
to leave off the dream.
"Mother," says he, "I saw a star
within my head in sleep just now *visioning of destroyment.*
that fell at me like Anu's dart
and I could not escape.

240   Uruk was on high of it,
our people did applaud,
and gathered up to praise his force.
Men clenched fists; women danced.
And I too embraced this rising star,
as a man does the woman he loves best,
then took the new one here to you
so that you could see us both at once."
Gilgamesh's mother, who is wise in all and worries not, replied:
"This bright, new star is your true friend

250   who fell at you like Anu's dart, *inevitable for*
whom you could not escape."

Column vi

Then she who is wise in all and worries not continued:
"So say this friend is one who is almighty,
with strength renowned around the world,
like Anu's dart his force is real
so that he draws you in, as does a spouse,
though he is sure to race away, like
that most distant star, with the secrets of your origin.
This dissolves your sleep."

260   Then again, Gilgamesh said to her in reply:
"Mother, I slept when some with axes then
attacked the herds of Uruk."
So Ninsun reassured the frightened king,
"Enkidu will help.
He will guard his loves
or rescue them from danger;

She let him see what force a woman has.
(figure 22)

he is your most faithful friend. *friend?*
Expect him to shepherd you
and to be sure that all goes well."

270   Gilgamesh said to his fond source:
"I pray for fortune and for fate
to send me such a one
that I may have a friend who's as kind
and patient as a brother."
Then in sleep full of repose
the temple priestess enchanted Enkidu
where they lay smiling.

Tablet II
Columns i – vi

The Meeting of Gilgamesh and Enkidu

Column i

Then Gilgamesh explained his dream to Ninsun:
"Last night a vision filled my head
with sights of stars and one sent down from heaven.
At first I tried and failed to carry forth
these signs with me. Then all citizens
of Uruk here assisted in my efforts.
So I was able then to bring these omens near to you."
And she said in reply:
"Wisely done, fair son, and rightly so
10   for one well reared as you were.
All others too will soon acclaim
this god-sent gift to you."
Then Gilgamesh concluded:
"In another dream I saw an ax
and bent toward it with manly interest;
so fair was its appearance
that it seemed wholesome, young and
ready as a woman."

Column ii

Soon the day came when the fine lover of Enkidu said:
20   "Now come with me to enter into Uruk
where we shall meet the mighty king,
enormous Gilgamesh.
Now you are as if a god,
with no more need of dumb beasts, however fair.
We can ascend the road to Uruk's palace,
the immaculate domicile, where Anu and Ishtar dwell
and there we will see Gilgamesh, the powerful,
who rides over the herd like any great king. → Similar people
You will see in him a power rare
30   and fairly learn to love him like yourself."

So the mighty brothers fought at first
pushing and shoving each other
for hours and hours enraged.
(figure 23)

They journeyed from the forest far and wide
to venture on toward Uruk.
The dispenser of Ishtar's sacrament led Enkidu
as gently as a mother would,
tearing her garment right in two
to hide their native beauty
and clothed his splendid body then
with her own cloak as they approached.

Column iii

Along the way he learned new human ways

[handwritten: → attacking beasts]

40 tracking down the gentle sheep
and using weapons for the first time
to fight away the savage beasts

[handwritten: becoming more human than animal]

that do attack the herds and
farms of men.

Column iv

Along the way he also learned to eat and drink
as men and women do. The Shamhat did
teach all these things too for Enkidu's first lessons.
And with a man upon the road they spoke
to learn of customs new to one from
50 far off woods. So Enkidu came then
to know of Gilgamesh who harshly
ruled and was not loved by those men whose wives
he often played with all night long.

And before they entered through the
gates of Uruk's mighty walls, Enkidu
was hailed as one who might
be sent to rival any king who
might treat gentle folk unfairly.

Column v

      In the alleys of Uruk
60   during a display of force
      the approach of Enkidu stopped everything.
      Uruk rose before him.
      The mountain beyond stretched skyward.
      All creatures worshiped him.
      Youths rallied round.
      People adored him as they adore a newborn babe.
      For so it is when one comes from nowhere
      to do what no one thought could be done.
      For Ishara then a wedding bed is set this night
70   because a guest has come who is as strong as any king.
      And Enkidu stood before the gate where new lovers go
      and stopped Gilgamesh from coming with nighttime lovers.
      It is there where they first fight
      throughout the night and round about Uruk's walls
      which they chipped and wrecked in places.

Column vi

      So the mighty brothers fought at first
      pushing and shoving each other
      for hours and hours enraged.
      Then a calm force gently soothed
80   their well-matched spirits
      to bring a peace and rest their strife.
      It was Enkidu who sued for rest saying:
      "Gilgamesh, enough! I am here to
      match some fate with you, not
      to destroy or rival any king."

              ↳ helping hand -"friend"

Tablet III
Columns i – vi

A Sacred Friendship Forged
The Plot to Conquer Humbaba

Column i

Then Enkidu and Gilgamesh joined in
sacred friendship and sealed their solemn
bond with noble kiss.

Column ii

Enkidu and Gilgamesh often sat then together,
visited Ninsun's shrine, conversed
of many plans and fashioned a future together.
Once, informed by fears of
future sorrow, Enkidu began
to weep and warn his friend of
10   coming horror. He said:
"If we go there beyond here to where
Humbaba-the-awful lives,
there will be a gruesome war
in a place no one calls home,
where no one wants to stay for long
or go to rest or rest to gain
the strength to reach the forests."
Ninsun rose within
and robed herself appropriately
20   covering herself,
ringing her curls beneath her crown
to ascend the altar, where she stood
lighting the first signals of charcoal for the incense
and preparing sacred cups that hold the
precious liquids which will be spilled.
Then Ninsun asked Shamash:
"Why?
Why have you called my only son away
and shaped his mind in so disturbed a way?
30   For now, he says, you invite him to begin a

[handwritten margin note: monster god who must be killed]

pilgrimage that ends where Humbaba
directs a never ending battle,
along a foreign, lonely road
far within the forests dark and damp
where a man like him might just kill
a god like Humbaba or be killed
to dissolve the pain that you, Shamash, oppose."

Column iii

Humbaba stirs within the darkened wood
and in the hearts of men there rises fear.
40 When Enkidu spoke at last to Gilgamesh
he said these words of warning:
"I knew this monster's reputation long ago.
Fire and death mix in his breath,
and I for one do not wish now
to challenge such a demon."
But Gilgamesh retorted: "All glory
will be ours if now we conquer
this unprecedented foe and risk the ⟶ *The venture to*
woe that frightens others."   *take down*
50 And Enkidu said then in swift reply: *Humbaba*
"How shall we go towards woods
so fiercely guarded?"

Column iv

Enlil it was who set Humbaba there
to scare away intruders with fierce
and frightening howls. Great Gilgamesh
remembered that when he spoke words like these
to Enkidu: "Only gods live forever
with Shamash, my friend; for even our
longest days are numbered. Why worry over
60 being like dust in the wind? Leap up for

this great threat. Fear not. Even if I were → *no fear in G.*
to fail and fall in combat,
all future clans would say I did the job."
Special weapons then were ordered to be made
for their assault upon Humbaba.
Axes, swords, and combat saddles were prepared
and all of Uruk's population flocked round
their great departure.

Column v

The awful monster's reputation
70   made Uruk's gentle people fear
for their great king. And after
all the plans were made to start
out to fight Humbaba, a group
came forward to see the king.
The elders spoke to Gilgamesh: → *G is un-wise in situation like these*
["Fear the force that you control, hot-headed one;]
Be sure you watch where you direct
your every, heavy swing in battle.
Vanguards protect.
80   Friends save friends.
Let Enkidu lead on the way
through forests that he knows.
He knows how to fight in woodlands;
he knows where to pick his fight.
Enkidu will shield his bosom too
as well as that of his companion
so as to protect them both.
He'll traverse any ditch of any width.
Enkidu will guard our king.   → *Guardian / protecter*
90   Be sure to bring him safely back."
Gilgamesh said to Enkidu:
"Arise, my other self, and speed your way to Egalmah
to where my mother sits, kind Ninsun.

She understands all I need to know.
She'll tell us where we should go and what to do."
Again the men embraced as teammates do.
Gilgamesh and Enkidu set out to Egalmah.

Column vi

Upset by all his thoughts of coming battles
and concerned by his consultations with the gods,
100 Gilgamesh then sadly set his palace rooms in order.
His weapons were prepared, his helmet shined
and garments freshly cleaned.
Citizens of Uruk came to say good-bye and
wish their daring king farewell.
"Go careful through this risky, bold adventure,
mighty lord. Be sure of your own safety first of all."
So spoke the elders of his town and then continued:
"Let Enkidu take risks for you and have him
lead the way through woods he knows so well.
110 Pray that Shamash show him, as your guide,
the nearest path and choicest route to
where you dare to go.
May great Lugalbanda favor you in combat with Humbaba."
Then Enkidu himself spoke finally to his king:
"The time is right for us now to depart.
Follow me, sir, along the savage way
to where a worthy opponent,
the awful beast Humbaba,
waits for your challenge in the
120 dark woodlands that he guards.
Do not fear this. Rely on me
in every matter and let me act
as careful guide for your most daring venture."

Humbaba stirs within the darkened wood
and in the hearts of ment there rises fear.
...Fire and death mix in his breath.
(figure 24)

Tablet IV
Columns i – vi

A Mother's Prayer
Journey to the Cedar Forest
An Ominous Wound

Column i, ii

First into the march, they stopped to eat.
   Next, they rested,
then finished another stretch that day.
Within three days they covered
what would take others a month and a half to travel.
They dug for water where
there appeared to be none
in the dry desert on their way
to challenge Humbaba.

Columns iii, iv

10 Onward ventured Gilgamesh and Enkidu
And they both knew where danger lurked
at their first destination.
As up they climbed upon the final hill,
they saw a guard put out by Humbaba
as fierce as any watchdog.
Gilgamesh pursued first.

Column v

Gilgamesh heard shouts from
Enkidu who said to his companion:
"Remember promises we made
20 in the city where we live. Recall
the courage and the force
we vowed to bring upon this mission."
These words dispelled the fear felt
in his heart and Gilgamesh in
return then shouted back:
"Quick. Grab the guard
and don't let go.

Race fearlessly and don't let go.
Our enemy, Humbaba, has set out seven uniforms
30 but has only dressed in one
so far. So six layers of strength
are yet unused by him."
As one mad brute he is enraged,
bellowing loudly while the foresters warn each other
what he's like.

Column vi

Wounded in combat with the guard they killed,
Enkidu uses words to say:
"I lost my strength in this crushed hand when the gate
    slammed shut.
What shall I do?"
40 Then Gilgamesh spoke: "Brother,
as a man in tears would,
you transcend all the rest who've gathered,
    for you can cry and kill
with equal force.
Hold my hand in yours,
and we will not fear what hands like ours can do.
Scream in unison, we will ascend
to death or love, to say in song what we shall do.
Our cry will shoot afar so
50 this new weakness, awful doubt,
will pass through you.
Stay, brother, let us ascend as one."

Tablet V
Columns i, iii, iv, vi

A Dream of Battle
Humbaba Slain

Column i

Gilgamesh and Enkidu froze and stared into the woods'
great depth and height. When they spied
Humbaba's path, they found the opening toward
straight passage. Then they were able to find and see
the home of the gods, the paradise of Ishtar's other self,
called Irnini-most-attractive.
All beauty true is ever there
where gods do dwell, where there is
cool shade and harmony and
10   sweet-odored food to match their mood.

Column iii

Then Gilgamesh envisioned yet again
another dream
high up in the hills
where boulders crashed.
Again Enkidu said to his brother,
as he unraveled this dreary story for his king:
"Brother, your song is a fine omen.
This dream will make you well.
Brother, that vision you saw is rich
20   for on that mountain top
we can capture Humbaba and
hurl his earthly form from
towering cliffs through sky to
earth, making his shape
as flat and wide as it is round and high."
"Mountain, that reaches into the sky,
humble this god with death."

Column iv

Mountain-on-high then sent the myth into Enkidu's sleep,
and a chill from the high winds forced him to rest,

30   since he was blown around as grain is on open field.
Curled up in a ball, Gilgamesh rested
in blessed sleep, the best of friends at the worst of times.
But by the moon's half way course, he rose
and then began to speak:
"Brother, if you made no noise, what sound woke me?
If you didn't jostle me, what shook my body?
There was no god nearby, so why am I so stunned?
Brother, I've had a third vision in sleep
and I am deeply frightened to recall it all.

40   Sky screamed. And Mother Earth moaned.
Sun went out of light and blackest night
enveloped the heavens.
Then came flashes of lightning, source of fire.
Storm clouds raced nearby and swept all life away
from out of the sky above our heads.
Brightness dissolved, light evaporated;
cinders turned to ash.
When we leave the mountain, this is what we will remember."
When Enkidu learned this myth as told,

50   he replied to Gilgamesh:
"Shamash, your god, creates a great attraction
for both of us. Shamash now approves
of this attack upon Humbaba. Take the sign
as some divine dream to urge us on."
Shamash himself said such words to Gilgamesh
as if in prayer:
"Do not balk now, favored one.
Brace yourself for battle and proceed."
Heavenly winds blasted down from out of the sky

60   about and all around Humbaba. From east and
west, with sand and grain, they blew him

back and forth. His giant self became
fatigued. His awesome strength dwindled.
Not even his great right foot could step away in flight.
So in this way, by Shamash's intervention,
Humbaba-the-awful beast was brought so low.

Column vi

The dying beast called out for mercy once
and part of what he said could still be heard over the
   howling winds:
"Please, Gilgamesh! Have mercy on me, wounded.
70   I shall freely give you all the lumber of my mighty realm
and work for you both day and night."
It was Enkidu then who shouted louder
than the beast and with his words he
urged a swift conclusion:
"Kill the beast now, Gilgamesh. Show
no weak or silly mercy toward so sly a foe."
Taking his companion's mean advice, Gilgamesh
swiftly cut the beast, splattering blood upon
his cloak and sandals then. Soiled by this
80   violent conflict, the friends began their
journey back to Uruk's towering walls
expecting now to be received as heroes who
had fought and won a legendary battle.

Tablet VI

Ishtar's Proposal

A Scathing Rejection

Ishtar's Revenge: The Bull of Heaven

The Slaughter of the Bull

Enkidu's Ominous Dream

Gilgamesh bathed himself and cleaned his hair,
as beautiful as it was long.
He cast off bloodied robes and put on his favorite gown,
secured the cincture and stood royal.
Then Gilgamesh put on his crown.
Ishtar looked up at Gilgamesh's handsome pride.
"Come to me," she whispered. "Come to me and be my groom.
Let me taste all parts of you,
treat you as husband, be treated as your wife.
10 And as a gift I'd give to you
one regal coach of gold and blue
with wheels of yellow and all so new
that I would flatter all your might
with the sight of demons driven off
by my own god, by my own man.
Come to my home, most sweetly scented of all places,
where holy faces wash your feet with tears as
do the priests and priestesses of gods like Anu.
All mighty hands of kings and queens
20 will open doors for you.
So too will all the countryside donate
in duplicate to your fold.
And the slow will race ahead for you,
so that by association, all that you touch
will turn to gold."
Gilgamesh replied to mighty Ishtar thus:
"But how could I repay you as a wife
and still avoid the bitterness and strife that follow you?"
Her tempting offer failed to trick the king
30 who feared to be ensnared by Ishtar's lust.
Instead, he taunted her with bitter words:
"So how am I to love you as you want
but still be free to roam or run at will?
If we tickled and teased or giggled and kissed,

we'd have no time to think clearly of all
the things non-lovers do who spend their time
better than those who play all day in bed.
Besides, I hardly know or trust you very much.
Here's a song I made for you
40   (a little rude, a little crude):
'Ishtar is the hearth gone cold,
a broken door that cannot hold,
a fort that shuts its soldiers out,
a commandant who'll only pout;
tar that can't be washed away,
a broken cup, stained and gray;
and worse than that or even this,
a god's own sandal filled with piss.
She's rock that's soft and useless.
50   She's fruit that's dry and useless.'
You've had your share of boys, that's true,
but which of them came twice for you?
Their stories I shall here repeat.
Tammuz, a virgin boy, did kiss Ishtar
and died within a week of meeting you.
Then you transferred lust to pets,
you turned your thoughts to raping beasts,
like birds or cats or little ducks,
each of which withered at your touch,
60   went blind or lame or mad or dumb.
You let a horse in your back door
by lying on a stable floor;
but then you built the world's first chain
to choke his throat and end his reign.
You let him run with all his might
as lovers sometimes do at night
before you harnessed his brute force
with labor mean, a cruel divorce.
So did his mother weep and wail
70   to see his hoof set with a nail.

...loose the bull who could trample him at once.
Let the bull spill his blood.
(figure 25)

Another time you saw a stranger
and thoughtless of impending danger
you toyed with him in naughty ways
to notch another trophy for
   your sexy reputation.
You fondled once a shepherd boy
who baked buns for your tongue's joy
and killed for you lamb after bleating lamb.
So in return for gifts like those
you chose to beastialize his toy.
80   And when his brothers saw his penis
they knew you'd done something heinous.
Can you recall Ishullanu
who trimmed your father's regal trees?
He worked each day with all his might
but couldn't stay awake at night.
You saw him in the midday sun
and his good looks forced you to say:
      'Hey, Ishullanu, how are you
      at plowing after hours?
90   Come, Ishullanu, into my bed.'
He balked. You sulked. And said that he
could find you hiding late that night
near elms within the royal gardens.
He said you knew he couldn't meet
to try to match your female heat,
so off he went instead to take his life.
These pets and people you destroyed
inform my view of how you act
so I will not make love with you."
100 When Ishtar heard him chide her so
she raced on high to Anu's star
where she whined: "Daddy, daddy, pleeeeease,
Gilgamesh called me a tease."
"Gilgamesh said I sinned and lived
without faith in myself or others," she pouted.

Her father, Anu, said these exact words to Ishtar:
"Now, daughter, did you first insult him,
this Gilgamesh who then began to taunt you
with jibes about your inclinations?"
110   Ishtar shouted back at him-who-is-her-father:
"You! Now! Make him stop! Loose the
bull who could trample him at once.
Let the bull spill his blood.
And you'd better do this now or I'll
wreak havoc of my own right down to hell.
I'll loose the goddamn devil. I'll rain corpses.
I'll make zombies eat infants and there will be
more dead souls than living ones!"
Her father, Anu, said these exact words to Ishtar:
120   "But if I do what you seem now to want,
there would be long years of drought
and sorrow. Have you stored enough
reserve to feed the people who
deserve your close protection?"
And she said:
"Yes, I have reserved a plan
for those I love. Now do as I demand
and punish all who insult me."
Then her father, Anu, heard Ishtar's cry
130   and Ishtar forced her will.
Anu set loose a bull from out of the sky and,
at the bull's proclamation, there cracks the
earth to swallow up nine dozen citizens of Uruk!
An earthquake fixed a grave for nine dozen citizens of Uruk.
Two or three or four hundred victims,
maybe more than that, fell into hell.
And when the quake returned for a third time,
it was near to Enkidu,
    he who fell upon the Abyss so wide and grim.
140   Enkidu collapsed near the earth-shaking bull.
Then he leaped to grab the bull by his long horns

even with spit upon his face from out the savage mouth,
even with the stench of bowels near his nose.
Then Enkidu said to Gilgamesh:
"Brother, you and I are now hailed as one.
How could we defeat a god?
Brother, I see great challenge here, but can we dare
    defy such force?
Let's kill it if we can right now.
Be unrelenting and hope that god
150 gives us the strength.
We must be cold and strong
to cut our enemy's weak neck."
Enkidu surrounds the bull, pursuing heaven's beast
and finally catches him.
So Gilgamesh, like a bull dancer,
svelte and mighty then,
plunged his sword into the throat held fast by Enkidu.
They butchered and bled the bull and then cut out its heart
to offer as sacrifice before Shamash.
160 Then Gilgamesh and Enkidu retreated
from the altar itself and stood afar
in deep respect as they did pray.
At last the two sat down, bound by war, bound by worship.
Ishtar appeared upon Uruk's walls
looking like a wailing widow.
She shrieked this curse aloud:
"Damn Gilgamesh, who injured me,
by slaughtering a divine bull."
Enkidu reacted to these words of Ishtar quick
170 by hurling at her head a hunk of meat from the bull's thigh.
And from afar he shouted up to her:
"This bloody mess of a plain bull would
be about what I could make of you
if you came near. I'd tie
your hands with these rope-like intestines."
Ishtar signaled then for her attendants:

coiffured bishops, cantors, and girls
whose charms keep worshippers coming.
Then atop the great wall above the city high
180 standing by the severed part of its right thigh,
she had them shriek laments for the bull who'd died.
So to complete this ritual and adorn his throne
Gilgamesh summoned artisans of all kinds.
Some measured the diameter of the bull's horns,
each containing thirty pounds of lapis lazuli.
Together those horns could hollow hold
half a dozen jars of oil.
And that is what Gilgamesh brought as potion
to the altar of Lugalbanda, his special protector.
190 He carried the horns and enshrined them in a place
of honor where his clan held rites.
Then Enkidu and Gilgamesh absolved their
bloody hands in the forgiving river,
the deep, eternal Euphrates that does not change.
At last relieved of such a stain, the friends renew
their vows with a brief embrace
before riding through Uruk's crowded streets
amid acclaim. There Gilgamesh stops to
give this speech to those gathered:
200 "What man is most impressive now?
Who is finest, firmest, and most fair?
Isn't Gilgamesh that man above men
and isn't Enkidu the strongest of all?"
Then they party loudly throughout the day
so that, come night, they drop down dead in sleep.
But Enkidu is resurrected quickly
to relieve his soul of fright
and sadly he asks Gilgamesh in tears:
"Oh brother, why would I dream that gods sat round
    to set my fate?"

Tablet VII
Columns i, iii, iv

The Death of Enkidu

Column i

E nkidu confessed this dream to Gilgamesh:
      "The gods all gathered round last night
and Anu told Enlil that one of us should die
because of what we've done against their names.
Though Shamash intervened for us,
saying we had slain Humbaba and the bull
with his consent, the others sought revenge."
Then Enkidu fell ill and soon lost his full strength.
Saying words like these as his friend lay dying,
10 Gilgamesh intoned:
"Why should you be so condemned and why should
I go right on living?
Will my own sad eyes soon never look on you again?
Shall I descend to depths beneath
this earth to visit worlds reserved
for those who've died?"
Enkidu glanced up, addressing the entryway
on which his hand was morbidly crushed:
"Door of all forests, that confuses wind and rain,
20 deaf, dumb, and blind portal;
I admired your firm texture
before I first saw the mighty trees
aloft that gave force to you.
There is nothing on earth that could replace
your splendor or your worth.
At two hundred feet in height, at forty feet around are
your mighty posts, your priceless hinge
cut and crafted in Nippur's holy ground.
If I had guessed that you'd become this,
30 I would have shattered you to pieces
with my ax and have been more careful not
to wound my hand so badly on your frame."

Column iii

Then cursing the hunter whom he first met
and the priestess whom he first loved, Enkidu raged:
"Slash him. Cut half his face.
Raise up floods beneath his feet
so that no animal is safe."
And at his sacred, former lover Enkidu did swear:
"Get up, witch, and hear your fortune
40   guaranteed now and forever.
I damn you off and damn you down.
I'd break your teeth with stones and let
your mouth hang open
until you'd say thanks to your killer
who would favor you by letting you
lie homeless on an open road
in some foul ditch.
May all and any who can hurt you now
often cross the paths you take. I
50   hope you live in fright, unsure of hope
and starved always for the touch of love."
Shamash responded from on high:
"The fine lover, my Enkidu, is cursed by you
who gave you bread and meat and stew,
the same who offered you some beer,
food and drink almost divine
so that you were taken for a god.
The fine lover, my thoughtless one, invested you
with robes of gold, robes of blue
60   and, more important, gave your dear friend
the thought that he should do whatever need
be done and still more too.
Did your brother, Gilgamesh, give you as fine a bed
as any on earth or any there in heaven?
Did he promote the likes of you to fame
unrivaled, so that rulers kneel to kiss

the ground you walk upon?
He will also show the Uruk people how to mourn for you.
An entire people will cry upon your death
70 and he will go in tears
ignoring the dirt and dust and mud
that stain his hands and hair.
So in despair will his mind be
as off he roams in lonely woods wearing rags."
When Enkidu heard these sad words
he was speechless and in his heart
he knew that Shamash spoke the truth.
His anger fled and Enkidu resolved
to die in peace.

Column iv

80 With these last words the dying Enkidu did pray
and say to his beloved companion:
"In dreams last night
the heavens and the earth poured out
great groans while I alone
stood facing devastation. Some fierce
and threatening creature flew down at me
and pushed me with its talons towards
the horror-filled house of death
wherein Irkalla, queen of shades,
90 stands in command.
There is darkness which lets no person
again see light of day.
There is a road leading away from
bright and lively life.
There dwell those who eat dry dust
and have no cooling water to quench their awful thirst.
As I stood there I saw all those who've died
and even kings among those darkened souls
have none of their remote and former glory.

100 All earthly greatness was forfeit
and I entered then into the house of death.
Others who have been there long
did rise to welcome me."
Hearing this, great Gilgamesh said to his handsome mother:
"My friend, dear Enkidu, has seen his passing now
and he lies dying here upon a sad and lonely cot.
Each day he weakens more and wonders how much more
life may yet belong to his hands and eyes and tongue."
Then Enkidu resumed his last remarks and said:
110 "Oh Gilgamesh, some destiny has robbed me
of the honor fixed for those who die in battle.
I lie now in slow disgrace, withering day by day,
deprived as I am of the peace that comes to one
who dies suddenly in a swift clash of arms."

Tablet VIII
Columns i – iii, v

Gilgamesh's Lament
The Specter of Mortality
Farewell to Enkidu

Column i

Then once again at break of day
    did Gilgamesh conclude the silent night
by being first to raise his hands and voice
and he said:
"Oh Enkidu, whose own mother's grace
was every bit as sweet as any deer's
and whose father
raced just as swift and stood as strong
as any horse that ever ran,

10   accept all natural customs
within the limitless confines of the wild
where you were raised by those with
tails, by those with hooves, by
those with fur and whiskers.
All the roads in and out of your great forest
now lie silent, but for the sobbing done by your wild friends.
The aged men and women of Uruk mourn today
and raise their withered palms in prayer
as we carry you by, toward Mount Kur.

20   Grottos weep for you and valleys too
and so do those great trees
upon the shore where you loved to run.
And also crying now are
large bears, little dogs, baby cubs
of lions and of tigers, and even
the hyena now has ceased its laugh.
Wild bull and the rapidest of deer
All, all, all sigh,
All, all, all cry for you.

30   Ulay's lovely riverbanks are swollen on this day
where you did walk as boys alone can do
upon the banks of rivers that mother
their young thoughts about life and death.
Yes, that great brown god, the river Ulay,

My friend has died and half my heart is torn from me.
Won't I soon be like him, stone cold and dead
for all the days to come?
(*figure 26*)

today mourns for you as does the
true Euphrates eternal and silent.
Uruk's rugged men mourn for you
who killed that sacrificial bull.
They all weep tears today
40   and those in Eridu, who loved your fame,
and say your name aloud,
they too weep tears today
and all in days to come, even those who knew
you not, all may weep tears someday
for your sad lot.
Your favorite aunt, your blessed servant,
your first girlfriend,
your inspiration, your companion, your darling
dear and she you feared to be alone with,
50   all women who ever sat and ate with you,
all men you ever helped with food or drink,
every one and all,
lovers fast and strangers slow.
Those you touched or who touched you
and those who never knew just how you felt.
All and every burst into tears
today because they heard that
you were suddenly dead."

Column ii

"I'll cry now, citizens of Uruk, and you
60   will finally hear what no one else
has ever had the nerve to say in sorrow.
I was family and friend to Enkidu and I shall
fill the woodlands where we stalked with loud, sad sobs today.
I cry now, Enkidu, like some crazed woman. I howl.
I screech for you because you were the ax upon my belt
and the bow in my weak hand; the sword within my sheath,
the shield that covered me in battle; my happiest robe,

the finest clothes I ever wore,
the ones that made me look best in the eyes of the world.
70 That is what you were; that is what you'll always be.
What devil came to take you off from me?
Brother, you chased down the strongest mule,
the swiftest horse on mountains high,
the quickest panthers in the flatlands.
And they in turn will weep for you.
Birds in the air cry aloud.
Fish in the lake gather together near the shore.
What else heeds this sorrow?
The leaves of the trees and the paths you loved
80 in the forest grow dark.
Night itself murmurs and so too does the day.
All the eyes of the city that once saw your kind
    face begin to weep.
Why? Because you were my brother and you died.
When we met and fought and loved,
we went up on mountains high to where we dared to capture
god's own strength in one great beast and then to cut its throat,
thus humbling Humbaba, green god of woodlands steep.
Now there is a sleep-like spell on you, and you
are dark as well as deaf."
90 Enkidu can move no more.
Enkidu can lift his head no more.
"Now there is a sound throughout the land
that can mean only one thing.
I hear the voice of grief and I know that you have been taken
somewhere by death.
Weep. Let the roads we walked together flood themselves
    with tears.
Let the beasts we hunted cry out for this:
the lion and the leopard, the tiger and the panther.
Let their strength be put into their tears.
100 Let the cloud-like mountain where you killed
the guardian of woodland treasures

place grief upon its sky blue top.
Let the river which soothed our feet overflow its banks
as tears do that swell and rush across my dusty cheeks.
Let the clouds and stars race swiftly with you into death.
Let the rain that makes us dream
tell the story of your life tonight.
Who mourns for you now, Brother?
Everyone who knew you does.

110 The harvesters and the farmers who used to bring you grain
are standing alone in their fields.
The servants who worked in your house
today whispered your name in empty rooms.
The lover who kissed every part of you
touches her chilled lips with scented fingers.
The women of the palace sit
and stare at the queen of the city.
She sobs and sobs and sobs.
The men with whom you played so bold

120 speak fondly of your name.
Thus they deal with this misfortune.
But what do I do? I only know that a cruel fate robbed me
of my dearest friend too soon.
What state of being holds you now? Are you lost forever?
Do you hear my song?"
"I placed my hand upon your quiet heart."
One brother covered the set face of another
with a bride-white veil.
"I flew above you then as if I were an eagle."

130 Then, like some great cat whose darling young have sadly died,
Gilgamesh slides back and forth fixed mindlessly on grief.
He commands many men to erect statues of honor, saying:
"Make his chest a noble blue and on his honored body
    place a jewel
as will allow all viewers then to see how great he was,
how great he'll always be."
Next day, Gilgamesh rose from a restless sleep.

Column iii

Then Gilgamesh continued with his bird-like words:
"On a pedestal I will honor your corpse
by setting you
140   above all earthly princes who will celebrate you
when people from all distant lands
both rich and poor in spirit
acclaim your memory.
And when you are gone,
never again to wear good clothes or care for food,
I'll still remember how you dressed and how you ate."
When day did break again next morn,
Gilgamesh stripped off the lion's cloak and
rose to say this prayer:
150   "Your funeral is a precious
gesture I made to hide my fearful guilt.
Goodbye, dear brother."

↔↔↔↔↔↔↔↔↔↔↔↔↔↔↔↔↔↔↔↔↔↔↔↔↔↔↔↔↔↔↔↔↔↔↔↔

—*Ave atque vale, frater.*
          — "Hail and farewell, Brother." (Latin)
—*Sat sri akai meri pra.*
          — "Goodbye, Brother." (Bengali: India)
—*Dehna hune wood wordema.*
          — "Farewell, sweet Brother." (Amharic: Ethiopia)
—*Slan agat, seanchara.*
          — "Go fairly, old friend." (Gaelic)
—*Shalom.*
          — "Peace." (Hebrew)

↔↔↔↔↔↔↔↔↔↔↔↔↔↔↔↔↔↔↔↔↔↔↔↔↔↔↔↔↔↔↔↔↔↔↔↔

Column v

Still grieving reverently
after he arose next day, Gilgamesh imagined the Annunaki
160 who decide the fate of
those who go to the underworld.
After learning how to pause his heart,
Gilgamesh created just the same image
in the face of a river.
At break of day,
on the sacred table made of special wood,
the grieving king placed a consecrated bowl of blue
filled with butter and with honey too
and this he offered up in solemn prayer
170 to Shamash, lord god.

Tablet IX
Columns i – vi

The Quest for Immortality
The Scorpion

so like a savage beast just then
did he bring death again and again
upon the lions' heads
(figure 27)

Column i

Then Gilgamesh wept some more
  for his dead friend. He wandered
over barren hills, mumbling to his own spirit:
"Will you too die as Enkidu did?
Will grief become your food? Will we both
fear the lonely hills, so vacant?
I now race from place to place,
dissatisfied with wherever I am and
turn my step toward Utnapishtim,
10 godchild of Ubaratutu,
who lives a pious life in fair Dilmun
where the morning sun arises as it
does in paradises lost and won.
As if in sleep I come upon the mountain door at midnight
where I face wild-eyed lions and I am afraid.
Then to Sin, the god of mighty light,
I raise my solemn chant to beg:
'Save me, please, my god.'"
Despite respite
20 he could not sleep or dream that night.
Instead he wandered through the woods
so like a savage beast just then
did he bring death again and again
upon the lions' heads
with an ax he drew
from off his belt.

Column ii

When he finally reached the base of
Mt. Mashu, Gilgamesh began to
climb the double cliff
30 that guides the rising and setting of Shamash.

Now these identical towers touch
the distant sky,
and far below, their breasts descend toward hell.
Those who guard the gate are
poison scorpions
who terrorize all, whose spells bring death.
And then resplendent power
thrives all across the town
where I was born
40   and rises farther still to
mountain tops.
At dawn and dark they shield Shamash.
And when he sensed them there,
Gilgamesh could not dare to look
upon their threat;
but held his glance away,
suspended fear,
and then approached in dread.
One among the guardians there
50   said this to his wife:
"The one who comes toward us
is partly divine, my dear."
And then the same one said
to the god-like part of Gilgamesh,
"Eternal heart, why make
this long, long trip
trying to come to us
through travail? Speak now."

Column iii

Gilgamesh said: "I come by here
60   to visit my elder, my Utnapishtim,
the epitome of both life everlasting and
death that is eternal."
The poison scorpion guardian said:

"No mortal man has ever
come to know what you seek
here. Not one of all your kind
has come so far, the distance
you would fall if you fell
all day and all night into the pit
70   and through great darkness
where there is no light
without Shamash who raises
and lowers the sun;
to where I let no one go,
to where I forbid anyone to enter."

Column iv

Heartachest pain abounds
with ice or fire all around.
The scorpion one,
I do not know whether a man or a woman,
80   said then:
"Gilgamesh, I command you
to proceed
to highest peaks
over hills toward heaven.
Godspeed!
With all permissions given here, I approve your venture."
So Gilgamesh set out then over
that sacred path within the mountains of Mashu,
near that incarnate ray of sunshine
90   precious to Shamash.
Oh dark, dark, dark, dark.
Oh the night, unholy and blind,
that wrapped him as soon as he stepped
forth upon that path.

So Gilgamesh set out then over
that sacred path within the mountains of Mashu,
near that incarnate ray of sunshine
precious to Shamash.
(figure 28)

Column v

DARKNESS
Beneath a moonless, starless sky,
Gilgamesh was frozen and unseeing
by time before midnight;
by midnight's hollow eye
100 he was unseen and frozen.
Initially he tripped and fell
blinded and frozen.
Next he staggered on
blinded and frozen.
Afterward he faltered not
blinded and frozen.
At dawn his second wind warmed him who still was
blinded and frozen.
And at your final dawn,
110 son of man, you will see only
a heap of broken images in an ascending
light that gives you sight you may not want,
for you will then behold all precious goods
and gardens sweet as home to you, as exile,
boughs of blue, oh unforgotten gem,
as true as any other memory from any other previous life.

Column vi

Then along the path
Gilgamesh traveled fast
and came at length to
120 shorelines fresh with dew.
And there he met a maiden,
one who knows the secrets of the sea.

Tablet X
Columns i – vi

Siduri whose Drinks Refresh the Soul

The Boatman, Urshanabi

Gilgamesh Implores Utnapishtim

Column i

This gentle one is called Siduri
    and she sits by the sea
where she sways from side to side.
She made the water pale; she crafted the first gold bowl
while peeking at the sun
through a slit across her face veil.
King Gilgamesh approached the woman's small cottage
    by the sea
dressed as a mountain man,
a meat-eater,
10 with an aching heart
and the stare of one setting out upon some
arduous, horrid trek.
She who gives her men lifesaving drinks
said to herself, "Beware of the one
coming now. He walks as if he'd kill."
And so Siduri locked the door,
put stones in place, lay on the floor.
When Gilgamesh heard sounds inside
he yelled at her. "Why do you hide?
20 Shall I have to break through this door?"
She whose drinks refresh the soul
then said these words to Gilgamesh:
"Is there a simple reason, sir, why you're so sad
or why your face is drawn and thin?
Has chance worn out your youth or did some
wicked sorrow consume you like food?
You look like one setting out on some arduous, horrid trek,
like one exposed to extremes of hot and cold,
like one who searches everywhere for grace."
30 He responded then to her who gives her men
lifesaving drinks:
"There is no simple reason why I'm so sad
or why my face is drawn and thin.

Chance alone did not wear out my youth. Some
wicked sorrow consumes me like food.
But I do look like one setting out on some
arduous, horrid trek, like one exposed
to extreme hot or cold,
like one who searches everywhere
40   for the breath of life
because my brother, my only true friend, met death;
he who raced wild horses there,
who caught orange tigers here.
This was Enkidu, my soul's good half,
who raced wild horses there,
who caught orange tigers here;
who did all things while he conquered mountains
and divine bulls that race
across the sky like clouds;
50   who gave Humbaba, the woodland god,
reason to weep when he stole through
the wooded path to slaughter lions."

Column ii

Gilgamesh continued:
"I greatly loved my friend who was always there for me.
I loved Enkidu who was always there for me.
What awaits us all caught him first
and I did thirst for one whole week to
see him once again in splendor until his body decomposed.
Then I wept for my future death
60   and I fled home for mountaintops to breathe
when my friend's death choked off my wind.
On mountaintops I roamed content to breathe
again when my friend's death choked off my wind.
Walking. Walking. Walking over hills.
Could I sit down to rest?
Could I stop crying then

when my best friend had died
as I will someday do?"
Then Gilgamesh said to the fair one
70 whose saving drinks gave life to men:
"Tell me how to get to Utnapishtim.
Where do I look for signs? Show me directions. Help.
Please let me have safe passage over seas.
Give me advice to guide me on my way."
She said to him in swift reply:
"No man has ever gone that way
and lived to say he crossed the sea.
Shamash only ventures there,
only Shamash would dare
80 to stare into the sun.
Pain joins the voyager soon,
and soon the traveler grows weary
where death surrounds the path
on every side with danger."

Column iii

She whose drinks refresh the soul
then said these words to Gilgamesh:
"Remember always, mighty king,
that gods decreed the fates of all
many years ago. They alone are let
90 to be eternal, while we frail humans die
as you yourself must someday do.
What is best for us to do
is now to sing and dance.
Relish warm food and cool drinks.
Cherish children to whom your love gives life.
Bathe easily in sweet, refreshing waters.
Play joyfully with your chosen wife."
"It is the will of the gods for you to smile
on simple pleasure in the leisure time of your short days."

Remember always, mighty king, that gods decreed the fate of all
many years ago. They alone are let to be eternal, while we frail humans die
as you yourself must someday do. What is best for us to do
is now to sing and dance. Relish warm food and cool drinks.
(figure 29)

100 "And what, after all, my fellow man,
would you do when you got to that
far side where Urshanabi dwells
among the hills of Utnapishtim?
He knows only the dead weight of what is dead
and he is one who plays with deadly snakes.
Would you put your lips near his?
If he befriends you then, go on.
But if he walks away, return to me."
With that in mind
110 Gilgamesh took up his chore,
unsheathed his sword, slipped toward the shore
and there joined one who rows the seas of death.
Gilgamesh sliced through the underbrush as an arrow goes
    through air
while cracking the stones of the sacred columns.
And Urshanabi barely saw the arrow's glint
and too late heard the ax's thud.
And so surprised was he that
there was never any chance to
hide or to deny the daring man
120 at least a chance at
some safe passage.
Gilgamesh traveled on to where he next
found the ferryman of Utnapishtim. This man,
Urshanabi, said to Gilgamesh:
"Your face seems tense; your eyes do not glance well
and hell itself is part of how you look.
Grief hangs from your shoulders.
You look like one who's been without a home, without a bed
or roof for a long time, wandering the wilds on some
    random search."
130 Gilgamesh replied to the ferryman:
"Yes sir, it's true my face is tense
and that my eyes seem harsh.
My looks are now so hellish,

for I wear my grief as ill as any other.
I'm not this way as some refugee
without a bed or roof for a long time,
and I don't wander the wilds randomly.
I grieve for Enkidu, my fair companion and true friend,
who chased the strongest mule, the swiftest horse
140   on mountain high, the quickest panther of the flatland.
Together we did all things, climbing sky-high peaks,
stealing divine cattle, humbling the gods, killing Humbaba
and the precious lions, guardians of the sky.
All this I did with my best friend who now is dead.
Mortality reached him first and I am left now
to weep and wail for his shriveling corpse which scares me.
I roam aloft and alone now, by death enthralled,
and think of nothing but my dear friend.
I roam the lonely path with death upon my mind
150   and think of nothing but my dear friend.
Over many seas and across many mountains I roam.
I can't stop pacing. I can't stop crying.
My friend has died and half my heart is torn from me.
Won't I soon be like him, stone-cold and dead,
  for all the days to come?"
Urshanabi replied as he had done before:
"Your face seems tense; your eyes do not glance well
and hell itself is part of how you look.
Grief hangs from your shoulders.
You look like one who's been without a home, without a bed
160   or roof for a long time, wandering the wilds on some
     random search."
And Gilgamesh said to him then in swift reply:
"Of course my face seems tense and my eyes seem harsh.
Of course I'm worn out weeping. Why should I not cry?
I've come to ask directions to Utnapishtim, who lives so
free beyond death's deep lake. Where can he be?
Tell me how to venture there where I may learn his secrets."
Finally, Urshanabi uttered these last words to Gilgamesh:

"You yourself have hurt this effort most, sir,
by blasphemy and sacrilege,
170   by breaking idols and by holding the untouchably sacred stones.
You broke stone images!
So now, raise high your ax."
Thus chastised, Gilgamesh
raised high his ax, unsheathed his sword,
did penance too as he chopped down many trees;
prepared them then, and then brought them
to Urshanabi.
After this, they cast off together,
with push and pull they launched the skiff
180   upon the waving sea.
They leaped quick, in three short days
covering a span that any other would
traverse only after months of passage
and soon they sailed on to Death's own sea.

Column iv

Still directing the king's new efforts, Urshanabi called:
"Pull, Gilgamesh, upon the mighty oar
and then pull another. Give ten times twenty
and then give twenty times ten pulls upon the
mighty oars; then ten more twice; then twice
190   more ten and then confuse the number of
the pulls you put upon the oar
by losing count aloud and starting over."
Half way through all that pulling,
Gilgamesh had worn the oars to bits
and torn his shirt from off his back
to raise a helping sail upon the mast.
Then Utnapishtim glared down from stars and clouds
and mused aloud, as if to coach the world:
"How could any human dare to break the idols
200   or steer the craft that gods and goddesses use?

Pull, Gilgamesh, upon the mighty oar and then pull another...
(figure 30)

This stranger is not fit to tie the shoes of servants.
I do see, but I am blind.
I do know, but cannot understand
how he behaves like
the beasts of here and there."

Column v

Gilgamesh spoke many words to Utnapishtim
and told of strife-in-life and
battles rare. He hailed his friend Enkidu,
acclaimed their pride and grieved the
210 death that saddened his great heart.
Gilgamesh raised his prayer to the remote Utnapishtim:
"Oh myth-filled god,
I have traveled many roads,
crossed many rivers and mountains.
I never rested. I never slept. Grief consumed me.
My clothing was ragged by the time I met
her who would help me.
I killed all manner of animal in order
to eat and clothe myself.
220 When I was rejected, I stooped to squalor.
Cursed I went,
being unholy."
Utnapishtim replied:
"Why cry over your fate and nature?
Chance fathered you. Your conception was
an accidental combination
of the divine and mortal.
I do not presume to know how to help
the likes of you."

Column vi

230 Utnapishtim continued:
"No man has ever seen Death.
No one ever heard Death's voice
but Death is real and Death is loud.
How many times must a home be restored
or a contract revised and approved?
How many times must two brothers agree
not to dispute what is theirs?
How many wars and how many floods must there be
with plague and exile in their wake?
240 Shamash is the one who can say.
But there is no one else who can
see what Shamash only can see within the sun.
Behold the cold, cold corpse from a distance,
and then regard the body of one who sleeps.
There seems no difference. How can we say
which is good and which is bad?
And it is also like that with other things as well.
Somewhere above us, where the goddess Mammetum
    decides all things,
Mother Chance sits with the Anunnaki
250 and there she settles all decrees of fable and of fortune.
There they issue lengths of lives;
then they issue times of death.
But the last matter
is always veiled from human beings.
The length of lives can only be guessed."
Thus spoke Utnapishtim.

Tablet XI
Columns i – vi

The Flood

Trial of Sleeplessness

Plant of Eternal Life

Foiled by the Serpent

Triumphant Return

Column i

To the most distant and removed of semi-gods,
    to Utnapishtim,
Gilgamesh said:
"When I regard you now, so godly a man,
it's like seeing my own face on calm water
where I dare to study myself.
Like me, you are first of all a fighter
who prefers to war-no-more.
How could one like you, so human, all-too-human,
ascend to be at one with other gods?"
10   Utnapishtim said to him in swift reply:
"Only one as bold as you would dare expect
such knowledge. But I shall tell you what
no person has ever been told.
High up the constant Euphrates
there rests a place you call Shuruppak
where gods and goddesses recline.
Then came the flood, sent by gods' intent.
Mama, Anu, and Enlil were at Shuruppak.
So too was their coachman, Ninurta,
20   and Ennugi, the bestiarius,
and one who watches over precious infants, the ever vigilant Ea.
And Ea refrained their chant to the high grown reeds
upon the shore, giving this advice to me:
'Arise! Arise! Oh wall-like reeds.
Arise and hear my words:
Citizen of Shuruppak, child of Ubaratutu,
abandon your home and build a boat.
Reject the stinking stench of wealth.
Choose to live and choose to love;
30   choose to rise above and give back
what you yourself were given.
Be moderate as you flee for survival
in a boat that has no place for riches.

Take the seed of all you need aboard
with you and carefully weigh anchor
after securing a roof that will let in no water.'
Then I said back in reverent prayer:
'I understand, great Ea.
I shall do just as you say to honor god,
40   but for myself
I'll have to find a reason to give the people.'
Then Ea voiced a fair reply:
'Tell those who'll need to know
that Enlil hates you.
Say: "I must flee the city now
and go by sea to where Enlil waits to take my life.
I will descend to the brink of hell
to be with Ea, god,
who will send riches to you like the rain:
50   all manner of birds;
birds...bords...burds...
and the rarest of rare fish.
The land will fill with crops full grown at break of day.
Ea will begin to shower
gifts of life upon you all".'"

Column ii

Then Utnapishtim continued saying words like these:
"By week's end I engineered designs
for an acre's worth of floor upon the ark we built
so that its walls rose straight toward heaven;
60   with decks all round did I design its space;
     120 cubits measured its deck.
With division of six and of seven
I patterned its squares and stairs;
left space for portals too,
secured its beams and stockpiled
all that ever could be used.

Pitch for the hull I poured into the kiln
and ordered three full volumes of oil
to start with and two times three more yet.
For what is security?
70   Each day I sacrificed the holy bulls
and chosen sheep for the people
and pushed the laborers to great fatigue
and thirst, allayed alone by wine
which they drank as if it were water running
from barrels set up for holding cheer
in preparation for a New Year's party they expected.
I set up an ointment box
and cleaned my fingers with its cream.
After one week, the ark was done,
80   though launching was more work than fun
since hull boards caught and snapped
until the water burst most of its great ton.
I supplied the craft with all I owned
of silver, gold, and seed.
My clan brought on the food they'd eat
and all the things we thought we'd need.
At last, it was my turn just then
to shepherd beasts and birds and
babies wet and loud.
90   It was Shamash who ordained the time, saying:
'Prepare the way for your whole boat
and set to sail when the storm
begins to threaten you.'
The Anunnaki too then cried for them.
The gods themselves, finally suffering, sat up
and let their first tears flow down
cheeks and over lips pressed closed.

Column iii

"For the whole next week
the sky screamed and storms wrecked the earth
100 and finally broke the war
which groaned as one in labor's throes.
Even Ishtar then bemoaned the
fates of her sad people.
Ocean silent.
Winds dead.
Flood ended.
Then I see a dawn so still;
all humans beaten to dirt
and earth itself like some vast roof.
110 I peeked through the portal into a morning sun
then turned, knelt and cried.
Tears flooded down my face.
Then I searched high and low for the shoreline,
finally spotting an island near and dear.
Our boat stuck fast beside Mt. Nimush.
Mount Nimush held the hull that could not sway
for one whole week.
I released the watch-bird, to soar in search of land.
The bird came back within a day
exhausted, unrelieved from lack of rest.
120 I then released a swallow, to soar in search of land.
The bird came back within a day
exhausted, unrelieved from lack of rest.
I then released a raven, to soar in search of land.
The bird took flight above more shallow seas,
found food and found release and found no
need to fly on back to me.
These birds I then released to earth's four corners
and offered sacrifice,
a small libation to the heights of many mountains,
130 from numbered chalices that I arranged.

Under these I spread the scents that gods favored
and when the gods smelled the sweet perfume of sacrifice,
they gathered in flight all above, like apparitions.

Column iv

"From distant heights with celestial views,
the female of all female gods descended then;
Aruru who aroused the wry thought
that Anu made for intercourse.
'Great Gods from far and wide
keep always in my mind
140   this thought for intercourse,
tokened by the sacred blue medallion on my neck.
Let me recall with smiles
these days in days to come.
Gods of my shoreline, gods of my sky,
come round this food that I prepared for you;
but do not let Enlil enjoy this too,
since he's the one who drowned my relatives
without telling the gods what he set out to do.'
When Enlil saw the boat, he released
150   his calm reason and let in the Igigi, monsters of blood.
'What force dares defy my anger!?
How dare a man be still alive!?'
Then with these words Ninurta said to Enlil:
'Can any of us besides Ea, maker of words,
create such things as speech?'
Then with these words Ea himself said to Enlil:
'Sly god,
sky darkener,
and tough fighter,
160   how dare you drown so many little people
without consulting me?
Why not just kill the one who offended you,
drown only the guilty?

I...offered sacrifice, a small libation...I spread the scents
that gods favored and when the gods smelled the sweet perfume of sacrifice,
they gathered in flight all above, like apparitions.
(figure 31)

Keep hold of his lifecord; harness his destiny.
Rather than killing rains, set cats at people's throats.
Rather than killing rains, set starvation on dry, parched throats.
Rather than killing rains, set sickness on the minds and hearts
    of people.
I was not the one who revealed our god-awful secrets.
Blame Utnapishtim,
170 who sees everything,
who knows everything.'"
"Reflect on these stories, my Gilgamesh."
"Then Enlil swooped down around my boat;
he gently raised me from the slime,
placed my wife beside my kneeling form
and blessed us both at once with hands upon our bowed heads.
So was it ordained.
So we were ordained."
Earlier than that time, Utnapishtim was not divine.
180 Then with his wife, he was deified
and sent to rule the place where rivers start.
"Gods sent me everywhere to rule the place where rivers start."
"As for you, Gilgamesh, which gods will be called on
to direct your path and future life?
Arise! Be alert! Stay up with stars for
seven long and sleepless nights!"
But even as he tried to stay awake,
foggy sleep rolled over his eyes.
Then Utnapishtim said these words:
190 "Dear wife, behold the one who tries to pray
while fog-like sleep rolls over his eyes."
She said to him who rarely talks:
"Arouse him now and let him
leave unharmed. Permit that one
to go back home at last."

Column v

Then Utnapishtim said these words:
"An upset soul can upset many gods.
Be kind with food and generous to him.
But keep a count of how he
200   sleeps and what he eats."
She was kind with food and gentle with the man
and she kept count of how he slept.
"One, two, three, alarie,
he slept with death-the-fairy.
Four, five, six, alarie,
he looked so cold and wary."
Then he returned from death to breath!
So Gilgamesh said to the One-who-rarely-spoke:
"Just as I slipped toward sleep,
210   you sent my dream."
And to him in reply, Upnapishtim said these words:
"You slept with death-the-fairy.
You looked so cold and wary.
Then you arose from death to breath."
So Gilgamesh said to the One-who-rarely-speaks:
"Help me, Utnapishtim. Where is
home for one like me whose self
was robbed of life? My own
bed is where death sleeps and
220   I crack her spine on every line
where my foot falls."
Utnapishtim calls out to the sailor-god:
"Urshanabi, dear, you will never land
again easily or easily sail the seas
to shores where you no more will find safe harbor.
Sandy and disheveled hair do not become
the one you nearly drowned.
Shingles now spoil his hidden beauty.
Better find a place to clean him up.

230   Better race to pools of saltless water soon
       so that today he'll shine again for all of us to see.
       Tie up his curly hair with ribbon fair.
       Place on his shoulders broad the happy robe
       so that he may return to his native city easily in triumph.
       Allow him to wear the sacred elder's cloak
       and see that it is always kept as clean
       as it can be."
       The sailor-god brought Gilgamesh
       to where they cleaned his wounds.
       By noon he shone again for all to see.
240   He tied his curly hair with ribbon fair,
       and placed upon his shoulder broad the happy robe
       so he would return to Uruk easily in triumph
       with a cloak unstained and unstainable.
       Urshanabi and Gilgamesh launched the boat
       over the breakers on the beach and
       started to depart across the seas.

Column vi

       To her distant husband, Utnapishtim's wife said:
       "This Gilgamesh has labored much to come here.
       Can you reward him for traveling back?"
250   At that very moment, Gilgamesh used paddles
       to return his craft along the shore.
       Then Utnapishtim called out to him:
       "Gilgamesh! You labored much to come here.
       How can I reward you for traveling back?
       May I share a special secret, one
       that the gods alone do know?
       There is a plant that hides somewhere among the rocks
       that thirsts and thrusts itself deep
       in the earth, with thistles that sting.
260   That plant contains eternal life for you."
       Immediately, Gilgamesh set out in search.

...but in the pool, a cruel snake slithered by
and stole the plant from Gilgamesh
who saw the snake grow young again
(figure 32)

Weighed down carefully, he dove beneath
the cold, cold waters and saw the plant.
Although it stung him when he grabbed its leaf,
he held it fast as he then slipped off his weights
and soared back to the surface.
Then Gilgamesh said this to Urshanabi, the sailor-god:
"Here is the leaf that begins
all life worth having.

270   I am bound now for Uruk,
town-so-full-of-shepherds,
and there I'll dare to give
this plant to aged men as food
and they will call it life-giving.
I too intend to eat it
and to be made forever young."
Next they ate.
Then they set up camp
where Gilgamesh slipped into a pool;

280   but in the pool, a cruel snake slithered by
and stole the plant from Gilgamesh
who saw the snake grow young again,
as off it raced with the miraculous plant.
Right there and then Gilgamesh began to weep
and, between sobs, said to the sailor-god who held his hand:
"Why do I bother working for nothing?
Who even notices what I do?
I don't value what I did
and now only the snake has

290   won eternal life. In minutes,
swift currents will lose forever
that special sign that god had left for me."
Then they set out again,
this time upon the land.
Next they stopped to eat.
Then they set up camp.
Next day they came to Uruk, full of shepherds.

Then Gilgamesh said this to the boatman:
"Rise up now, Urshanabi, and examine
300 Uruk's wall. Study the base, the brick,
the old design. Is it permanent as can be?
Does it look like wisdom designed it?
The house of Ishtar in
Uruk is divided into three parts:
the town itself, the palm grove, and the prairie."

Place on his shoulders broad the happy robe
so that he may return to his native city
easily in triumph.
(figure 33)

Tablet XII

Descent to the Underworld
The Afterlife

Introduction to Tablet XII

Scholars disagree about the relation of Tablet XII to the other eleven tablets. The general consensus is that it was an appendage added to the other Gilgamesh stories at a later date. This tablet presents a stark contrast to the earlier eleven in style and narrative. The appearance of a "resurrected" Enkidu is especially startling. In light of these inconsistencies, why include Tablet XII?

Tablet XII provides further insight into some of the major themes and questions explored in the first eleven tablets. Is there an afterlife? What is the nature of it? What earthly behaviors are rewarded there? By the conclusion of Tablet XI, Gilgamesh was forced to accept the limits of mortal existence and be satisfied with its attainable rewards. Questions about the "state of being" in death had fiercely possessed him, however, and the answers remained a mystery. This defining and "coming to terms" with human mortality has been the province of every system of religious beliefs throughout history. Here is our first recorded vision of afterlife. It is for these reasons that Tablet XII is included in this edition of the epic.

"If only I'd have protected our instruments in the
 safe home of the drum-maker;
If only I'd have given so precious a harp to the
craftsman's wife, she who shepherds such jewel-like children.
God, has your heart forgotten me?
Who shall descend to hell and redeem the
drum from where it rests unused?
Who shall risk his life to retrieve
the precious gifts of Ishtar from death?"
10   And for this quest his friend alone did pledge.
So Gilgamesh said this to Enkidu:
"Descend, descend to hell where life does end
but listen now to words you need to know.
Go slow to where death rules, my brother dear,
and then arise again above and over fear."
And, once more, Gilgamesh said this to Enkidu:
"Let all who would be saved today, take heed,
and listen to god's words in time of need.
When walking with the strong or with the dead,
20   do not wear clothes of purple or of red.
Shun make-up that presents a holy face
for they attack the phony and the base.
Leave here with me your knife and rock and club;
such weapons only add to their own strife.
Put down your bow, as you would leave a wife.
The souls of death will soil your hands and feet.
Go naked, filthy, tearful, when you meet.
Be quiet, mild, remote, and distant too
as those who will surround and follow you.
30   Greet no girl with kiss so kind upon her lips;
push none away from you with fingertips.
Hold no child's hand as you descend to hell
and strike no boy who chooses there to dwell.
Around you, Enkidu, the lament of the dead

will whirl and scream,
for she alone, in that good place, is at home who,
having given birth to beauty,
has watched that beauty die.
No graceful robe any longer graces her naked self
40 and her kind breasts, once warm with milk,
have turned into bowls of cold stone."
But Enkidu refused to heed his friend
as he set out that day to then descend
to where the dead who-do-not-live do stay.
He wore bright clothes of celebrative red,
the sight of which offended all the dead.
His colored face made him seem fair and good
but spirits hate the flesh that would dare
remind us of the beauty they have lost.
50 He brought with him his club and rock and knife
and did cause strife with those whom he did mock.
There, too, is where he showed off;
where he went clothed among the naked,
where he wasted food beside the starving,
where he danced beside the grief stricken.
He kissed a happy girl.
He struck a good woman.
He enjoyed his fatherhood.
He fought with his son.
60 Around him, the lament for the dead arose;
for she alone, in that sad place, is at home who,
having given birth to beauty,
has watched that beauty die.
No graceful robe any longer graces her naked self
and her kind breasts, once warm with milk,
have turned into bowls of cold stone.
She never even dreamed once of letting him return
to life. Namtar, the decision-maker,
would not help Enkidu. Nor would illness
70 help. Hell became his home.

Nergal, chief-enforcer, would not help.
Dirges and laments rose all around.
Not even the soldier's death-in-battle,
with all its false and phony honor,
helped Enkidu. Death just swallowed him, unrecognized.
So the great son of Ninsun, proud Gilgamesh,
cried for his beloved friend
and went to the temple of Enlil,
the savage god of soldiers,
80   to say: "My god, when death
called for me, my best friend went
in my place and he is now no longer living."
But the savage god of soldiers, Enlil, was mute.
So Gilgamesh turned next to one who flies alone,
and to the moon he said: "My god, when death
called for me, my best friend went
in my place and he is now no longer living."
But the moon, who flies alone, was also mute;
so he went next to Ea, whose waters fill
90   the desert oasis even when no rain falls.
"My god," he cried, "when death
called for me, my best friend went
in my place and he is now no longer living."
And Ea, whose waters keep us alive as we journey
        over desert sands,
said this to Nergal, great soldier in arms.
"Go now, mighty follower; free Enkidu to speak once to kin
and show this Gilgamesh how to descend halfway
to Hell through the bowels of earth.
And Nergal, accustomed to absurd orders,
100   obeyed as soldiers do.
He freed Enkidu to speak once to kin
and showed Gilgamesh how to descend halfway
to Hell through the bowels of earth.
Enkidu's shadow rose slowly toward the living
and the brothers, tearful and weak,

tried to hug, tried to speak,
tried and failed to do anything but sob.
"Speak to me please, dear brother,"
whispered Gilgamesh.

110 "Tell me of death and where you are."
"Not willingly do I speak of death,"
said Enkidu in slow reply.
"But if you wish to sit for a brief
time, I will describe where I do stay."
"Yes," his brother said in early grief.
"All my skin and all my bones are dead now.
All my skin and all my bones are now dead."
"Oh no," cried Gilgamesh without relief.
"Oh no," sobbed one enclosed by grief.

120 "Did you see there a man who never fathered any child?"
"I saw there a no-man who died."
"Did you see there a man whose one son died?"
"I saw him sobbing all alone in open fields."
"Did you see there a man with two grown sons?"
"I did indeed and he smiles all day long."
"Did you see there a man with three of his own boys?"
"I did, I did; and his heart's full of joys."
"Did you there see a king with four full kids?"
"I did see one whose pleasure is supreme."

130 "Did you see there anyone with five children?"
"Oh yes, they go about with laughs and shouts."
"And could you find a man with six or seven boys?"
"You could and they are treated as the gods."
"Have you seen one who died too soon?"
"Oh yes; that one sips water fair and rests
each night upon a couch."
"Have you seen one who died in War?"
"Oh yes; his aged father weeps and his young widow
    visits graves."
"Have you seen one buried poor, with other homeless nomads?"

140 "Oh yes; that one knows rest that is not sure,

far from the proper place."
"Have you seen a brother crying among relatives
who chose to ignore his prayers?"
"Oh yes; he brings bread to the hungry from
the dumps of those who feed their dogs
with food they keep from people
and he eats trash that no other man would want."

GLOSSARY

The following people, gods, goddesses and places are mentioned in this edition of *The Epic of Gilgamesh.* Since there is no scholarly certainty about the pronunciation of some of the terms, phonetic pronunciations assimilated from various sources are included here. These do not pretend to be the final word — merely a device to help the reader experience a fluid reading, unhampered by the otherwise inevitable stumbling over unfamiliar terms.

Anu (ah´ noo) - father of the gods and sky god associated with all heavenly wonder, father of Ishtar. The city of Uruk was sacred to him.

Anunnaki (ah noo nah´ kee) - spirit gods of the underworld who judged and determined the fates of the dead.

Aruru (ah roo´ roo) - great mother goddess of creation who molds Enkidu from clay in the images of Anu and Ninurta. She is also called Mammetum in her role of decreeing destinies.

Dilmun (deel´ moon) - paradise regained, land where the sun rises, where the deified Utnapishtim settled after surviving the great flood.

Ea (ay´ ah) - god of water and wisdom, protector of human beings, his breath-born words encourage hope. He is also called Enki.

Eanna (ay ahn´ ah) - the sacred temple of Anu and Ishtar in the city of Uruk.

Egalmah (ay´ gahl mah) - the sacred temple of Ninsun in the city of Uruk.

Enkidu (en´ kee doo) - a "natural" man created by Aruru, modeled after Anu and Ninurta, to become a rival then friend/alter ego to Gilgamesh. He is introduced to civilization by his union with Shamhat, the sacred temple priestess.

Enlil (en´ lil) - god of earth, wind and air associated with the savage arts of soldiers. He sent the great flood that drowned all but

Utnapishtim and his family and sent Humbaba to guard the cedar forest.

Ennugi (en noo´ gee) - minor gods or demons

Euphrates (you fray´ teez) - river originating in the mountains in the north of Turkey and emptying into the Persian Gulf after joining the Tigris. Ancient Mesopotamia, "The-land-between-two-rivers," derives its name from its location between the Euphrates on the west and the Tigris on the east and is believed to be the cradle of civilization.

Gilgamesh (gil´ gah mesh) - hero of the epic, son of the goddess Ninsun and possibly former king of Uruk Lugalbanda. His insatiable appetites and unbridled behavior drive his subjects to seek help from the gods to divert his overabundant energies from their sons, daughters, and brides. Gilgamesh is an historic figure, as well as the legendary hero of a number of ancient tales.

Humbaba (hoom bah´ bah) - nature god, assigned by Enlil to oversee the cedar forest, slain by Gilgamesh and Enkidu. He is also called Huwawa.

Igigi (ee gee´ gee) - collective name for the great gods of heaven associated with blood, madness and revenge, often associated with the Anunnaki.

Irkalla (ear kahl´ lah) - a name for the underworld, also used in place of Ereshkigal who is queen of the underworld and wife of Nergal.

Ishara (ee shah´ rah) - see Ishtar.

Ishtar (eesh´ tar) - goddess of love and sexuality, also of war, patron of Uruk with her father Anu. She wrought deadly havoc after her rejection by Gilgamesh. She is called Ishara in her role during the sacred ritual of marriage, and is also called Inanna and Irini.

Ishullanu (ee shoo lah´ noo) - gardener of Anu, one of the many discarded lovers of Ishtar.

Lugalbanda (loo gahl bahn´ dah) - shepherd and early king of Uruk, thought to be the father of Gilgamesh. He was later deified.

Mt. Mashu (mah´ shoo) - twin peaks representing the place where the sun would rise and fall.

Mt. Nimush (nee´ moosh) - peak on which Utnapishtim's ark came to rest, formerly called Nisir.

Namtar (nahm´ tahr) - underworld demon linked with fate as a negative destiny.

Nergal (near´ gahl) - chief god of the underworld responsible for plagues, chief enforcer and soldier-in-arms.

Ninsun (neen´ soon) - wise goddess, mother of Gilgamesh, wife of Lugalbanda. Her name means "lady wild cow."

Ninurta (neen oor´ tah) - god of war and agriculture, associated with the south wind. Enkidu is created partially in his image.

Nippur (nee poor´) - city sacred to Enlil, religious capital of ancient Mesopotamia.

Nisaba (nee sah´ bah) - goddess of grain, often depicted with hair of breeze-blown grain. Enkidu's hair resembled hers.

Shamash (shah´ mahsh) - sun god and god of justice who despises evil. He encourages Gilgamesh to destroy Humbaba and protects him in the endeavor.

Shamhat (shahm´ haht) - sacred priestess most likely from the temple of Ishtar who brings civilization to Enkidu through her union with him.

Shuruppak (shoo´ roo pahk) - an ancient city of Sumer located north of Uruk, former home of Utnapishtim from where the gods issued the great flood.

Siduri (see door´ ee) - barmaid who lives near the salvific shore. She advises Gilgamesh to abandon his quest for immortality and enjoy the temporal pleasures allotted to mortals while he may.

Sin (seen) - moon god.

Tammuz (tahm´ mooz) - shepherd of Uruk, god of vegetation, virgin boy until his union with Ishtar, then another of her discarded lovers. He is also called Dumuzi.

Ubaratutu (oo bahr ah too´ too) - god and father of Utnapishtim, former king of Shuruppak.

Ulay (oo lie´) - river where Gilgamesh and Enkidu rested.

Urshanabi (oor shah nah´ bee) - ferryman and sailor god whose boat crosses the waters separating the garden of the sun from the paradise where the deified Utnapishtim lives. He conveys Gilgamesh to Utnapishtim.

Uruk (oo´ rook) - ancient city on the Euphrates River, a center of Sumerian culture circa 3000 B.C., kingdom of Gilgamesh and sacred to Anu and Ishtar.

Utnapishtim (oot nah peesh´ teem) - legendary survivor of the great flood who was granted immortality. Gilgamesh seeks from him the secret of eternal life. He is also called Ziusudra.

Why Gilgamesh?

The Great Books Foundation has declared
The Epic of Gilgamesh a classic by adding it
to the list of "Great Books."

Archaeologists in Iraq believe they have found the tomb of King
Gilgamesh, the subject of the world's oldest "book."

http://news.bbc.co.uk/go/em/fr/-/2/hi/science/nature/2982891.stm

http://www.wikipedia.org/wiki/Epic_of_Gilgamesh

"... one of humanity's most magnificent
poems ..."
— Frederick Goldin,
City College of New York

"... the ancient prototype for the
development of civilization ..."
— Dr. E. Otha Wingo,
Southeast Missouri State University

"... an integral part of the literary and
mythological environment of the ancient
world ..."
— Pamela Vaughn,
California State University, Fresno

BOLCHAZY-CARDUCCI PUBLISHERS, INC.
www.BOLCHAZY.com

The Genesis of Literature

- One of the First Extant Epics
- One of the First Euhemeristic Heros
- One of the First Accounts of the Search for Immortality
- Some of the First Biblical Archetypes
  - The Civilization of the Noble Savage
  - Adam and Eve Myth
  - The Flood
  - The Serpent
- First Mythology in the Form of Literature in an Extant Ancient Work

The Existentialist Focus

- 1st Stage: Hormonal
- 2nd Stage: Intimacy
- 3rd Stage: Empire Building
- 4th Stage: Awakening
- 5th Stage: Fear of Death
- 6th Stage: Derangement
- 7th Stage: Quest for Immortality
- 8th Stage: Resignation

First Set of Women in Literature

- Shamhat—Ishtar—Siduri—Wife of Utnapishtim
- Shamhat, prototype of Eve, civilizes Enkidu, rival and alter ego of Gilgamesh, through the sacrament of Ishtar.
- Ishtar, powerful goddess and seductress, brings tragedy to Gilgamesh and Enkidu through her wrath.
- Siduri, prototype of Sapientia, serves Gilgamesh soothing drink and promulgates the ultimate goal of human life.
- Wife of Utnapishtim, urges Utnapishtim to share the herb of immortality with Gilgamesh.

Topics of Reference

- Conflict and reconciliation of opposites: savage—civilized, life—death, shadow—ego
- The relevance of dreams to the narrative, to Myths and to personal development
- Biological and psychological evolutions, a journey into the past in search of an inner future
- The importance of coping with danger: Gods, Monsters, Trees—the meaning of symbols
- The relationship between conscious and the subconscious as to their influence on mental development
- The existential stages in a human being
- Mythological parallels

THE EPIC OF GILGAMESH
A Myth Revisited

198 pp. (2002) Deluxe Case Bound ISBN 978-0-86516-527-4

A Timeless Tale...
A Stunning Tome

Bilingual Edition: Hebrew and English

A brilliant and compelling work of art—this book offers:

- Saul Tchernichovsky's classic Hebrew translation of The Epic of Gilgamesh
- The Epic of Gilgamesh in English verse, by Danny P. Jackson
- Brilliant, full-color illustrations by Zeev Raban, with commentary*
- "The Epic of Gilgamesh As A Journey of Psychological Development" by David S. Kahn
- "Gilgamesh, An Appreciation" by James G. Keenan

"The Epic of Gilgamesh is often regarded as the first piece of world literature. Even after four thousand years, it still reaches all of us, wrestling as it does with basic questions of the meaning of life and death. New translations, retellings and studies of *Gilgamesh* appear every year, directed to scholars, to a more popular audience, and even to children.

This volume is meant for a popular audience. It includes a translation into English, by Danny P. Jackson, and one into Hebrew, by the poet Saul Tchernichovsky. Both translations, but particularly that of Jackson, are rather free renderings of the text, not literal translations. The book is prefaced by articles (each in both English and Hebrew) which explore the psychological dimensions of *Gilgamesh*. The heart of the volume are fourteen gouache paintings by Zeev Raban, never previously published, which illustrate events of the narrative. The colors in these paintings are stunning.

This is a handsome, even sumptuous volume, one which it is a pleasure to touch and to read. The translations are printed over colors and patterns drawn from Raban's paintings.

Specialists will argue over nuances of the translations. The true test of a classic is that each time one reads it, one finds something new, and that is true of these translations."

– Dr. John Hayes, Near Eastern Studies,
University of California, Berkeley

Dr. Hayes will be publishing a longer and more scholarly review of this title in a forthcoming issue of the *Journal of Near Eastern Studies*.

Published by Bolchazy-Carducci Publishers, Inc. and D. K. GraubArt Publishers Ltd.

*See: www.BOLCHAZY.com/gallery/gilgslideshow/mgilgslide.html for gallery

BOLCHAZY-CARDUCCI PUBLISHERS, INC.
WWW.BOLCHAZY.COM

THE EVOLUTION OF
THE GILGAMESH EPIC

Jeffrey H. Tigay

xvii + 384 pp. (2002, Reprint of 1982 University of Pennsylvania Press Edition) Paperback, ISBN 978-0-86516-546-5

"Tigay's work of 1982 stands as an important milestone in the history of Gilgamesh studies...the work of the last twenty years makes clear the importance of his approach and of the topics which he studied. This welcome reprint...will surely stimulate and serve a new generation of scholars and students."

– Tzvi Abusch, from the book's new Foreword

Contents

"[Tigay's] book will prove a most useful and most important tool for further scholarly advance. I can warmly recommend its publication."

– Thorkild Jacobsen, emeritus, Harvard University

"This important book, [is] rich in detail and elaborate in presentation... scholars of literature, of the history of religions, of biblical studies, or, for that matter, devotees of Gilgamesh and his legends will find the book rewarding."

– Jack M. Sasson, *Religious Studies Review*

"I think that this is a first-class piece of scholarship... [Tigay] has given us the first comprehensive analysis of the post-Sumerian Gilgamesh material, has examined in detail the interrelationships within this material, and has presented a strong case for a certain line of development."

– William L. Moran, Harvard University

"There is no doubt that the reading and study of this carefully prepared work is to be recommended not only to Assyriologists and biblical scholars, but to all those who are seriously interested in the culture of the ancient Near East, in the history of literature and religion, or simply in one of the most outstanding expressions of humanism."

– E. Lipinski, *Israel Exploration Journal*

"This is an important book for understanding the Gilgamesh epic itself."

– Theodore J. Lewis, *Hebrew Studies*

"Jeffrey Tigay's exposition is an exhaustive treatise whose method and meticulous scholarly approach is founded upon textual evaluations rather than hypothetical literary criticisms."

– L. M. Young F. R. A. I., *Wiener Zeitschrift für die Kunde des Morgenlandes*

"Tigay's major study replaces the short article by S.N. Kramer on the development of this Mesopotamian literary composition . . .The book is essential for all who would study the Gilgamesh Epic."

– W. R. Bodine

BOLCHAZY-CARDUCCI PUBLISHERS, INC.
www.BOLCHAZY.com

GILGAMESH A READER
Interpretive Studies on Gilgamesh
John Maier, Ed.

Illus., 504 pp. (1997)
Hardbound, ISBN 978-0-86516-349-2, Paperback, ISBN 978-0-86516-339-3

Gilgamesh: A Reader is a collection designed to
• enrich the reader's background information on the epic • help draw connections between Gilgamesh and other literature • stimulate thought and descussion • enliven interest in Gilgamesh

Intended for general readers, teachers, and students of *The Epic of Gilgamesh*

Contents of *Gilgamesh: A Reader*

BOLCHAZY-CARDUCCI PUBLISHERS, INC.
WWW.BOLCHAZY.COM

THE EPIC OF GILGAMESH

By Danny P. Jackson; Illustrated by Thom Kapheim

lxii + 106 pp. (2008) Paperback ISBN 978-0-86516-352-2

Danny P. Jackson's rendition of *The Epic of Gilgamesh*, first published by Bolchazy-Carducci Publishers in 1992, has gained recognition in the publishing world.

First, it was chosen by Prentice Hall for their anthology, *Literature of the Ancient World*, vol. I (New York, 2000).

Then, one year later, fine art publisher D.G. GraubArt Publishers chose Jackson's rendition from among many others for their lavishly illustrated Hebrew/English edition, *The Epic of Gilgamesh: A Myth Revisited* (Jerusalem and Wauconda, 2001).

In 2004, the Great Books Foundation added the Jackson's rendition of *The Epic of Gilgamesh* to its adult book series.

Now available in Turkish.

Bolchazy-Carducci Publishers is proud to have the merit of Jackson's accessible, poetic rendition recognized by three other publishers.

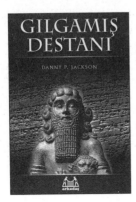

GILGAMIŞ DESTANI
The Epic of Gilgamesh in Turkish

By Danny P. Jackson; Illustrated by Thom Kapheim
Translated by Ahmet Antmen

lxiv + 94 pp. (2005) Paperback ISBN 975-509-440-7

The Turkish edition of the Gilgamesh, *Gilgamiş Destani*, is a faithful translation of Jackson's rendition. This first translation in Turkish contains the entire content of the Bolchazy-Carducci Publishers edition: Introduction by Robert D. Biggs; Appreciation by James G. Keenan; eighteen photographs of artifacts, captioned by Robert D. Biggs; 'My Poetic Intention' by Danny P. Jackson; all twelve tablets of the Gilgamesh text; glossary of proper names; and fifteen original woodcuts by Thom Kapheim.

Though *The Epic of Gilgamesh* exists in several editions, Bolchazy-Carducci's version was undertaken with a very specific intent—to remain faithful to the source material while attempting to convey the poetic scope of a work that is both lusty and tender and one that retains the ability to arouse compassion and empathy in all who follow Gilgamesh on his journey. This edition reanimates the story of Gilgamesh and Enkidu for modern readers through indelible poetic images.

BOLCHAZY-CARDUCCI PUBLISHERS, INC.
www.BOLCHAZY.com